SAMANTHA PARSONS & JOHN BYNNER

INFLUENCES ON ADULT BASIC SKILLS

Factors affecting the development of literacy and numeracy from birth to 37

Social Statistics Research Unit, City University

Published March 1998

ISBN 1 85990 076 3

Design: Studio 21

Contents

Tables

Figures

Summary

Basic Skills are essential to functioning in most areas of modern life. Those whose basic skills are poor suffer from a wide range of disadvantage, becoming increasingly marginalised in their working lives and in their role as citizens. Men tend to drift into unskilled casual jobs and unemployment; women leave the labour market early, often to have children. Their lives are characterised by lack of opportunity and depression. To reverse the cycle of difficulty we need to know how these problems originated and what influences later in life serve to counter them.

This report presents the results of a study of the influences on basic skills, from birth to 37, in a sample of 1700 people. They were born in 1958 and are part of the National Child Development Study. This study builds on earlier work on a comparable sample born in 1970 in which it was possible to trace the basic skills acquisition process only up to the age of 21[1]. In the study covered by this report, each cohort member was interviewed at age 37 about their work, family life, health and well-being. At the end of the interview the cohort members completed tests of functional literacy and numeracy, from which it was possible to classify them in terms of four literacy and numeracy groups, 'very low', 'low', 'average', and 'good'. Our first report, *It doesn't get any Better*[2], compared the circumstances and experiences of people in each of the four groups, and the impact of poor basic skills on their lives. This study looks behind the problems the survey revealed. It examines the factors that appear to be most influential in an emerging pattern of poor basic skills. It also seeks to find out what kinds of interventions at different stages in life are most likely to succeed in preventing basic skills difficulties.

The influences on basic skills are examined under headings describing the stages of life in which they occur: Family and Home Circumstances; Early Education and Schooling; Transition from School to Work, Adult Working Life. We use statistical

---

1. *Difficulties with Basic Skills*, Bynner, J. and Steedman, J., Basic Skills Agency, 1996.
2. Bynner, J. and Parsons, S., Basic Skills Agency, 1997.

analysis to see how powerful all the influences taken together are in explaining literacy and numeracy performance at age 37, and to find out which of them are the most critical.

Findings

Family and Home Circumstances

Poverty and disadvantaged circumstances were more evident in the childhood of the adults with basic skills difficulties and their parents were the least likely to have experienced post-16 education. Books were also less common in their homes when they were children.

- Adults with very low literacy were seven times more likely to have received free school meals at age 11 when compared with adults who had good literacy (28% to 4%); adults with very low numeracy were six times as likely to have received free school meals in comparison to those with good numeracy (19% to 3%).

- Adults with very low literacy or very low numeracy were twice as likely to have grown up in Council rented accommodation when compared with adults who had good skills (55% to 26% by literacy), and were at least three times as likely to share their bedroom with 2+ other family members at age 11 (34% to 9% by literacy; 24% to 8% by numeracy).

- No more than 1 in 8 mothers or fathers of cohort members with either very low literacy (10% mothers, 13% fathers) or very low numeracy (12% mothers, 13% fathers) had participated in post-16 education. By contrast, 1 in 3 parents of cohort members with good skills (30% mothers and fathers by literacy; 36% mothers, 37% fathers by numeracy) remained in education after they were 16.

Early Education and Schooling

The whole education experience of adults with basic skills difficulties differed from that of adults with good literacy and numeracy. They were the least likely in the cohort to have been read to as a child. As reported by teachers, they were less likely to have experienced teaching of phonics (letter sounds) and basic numberwork by age 5½. They attended schools where academic achievement and future aspirations were relatively low. Cognitive ability tests taken at 7 showed that adults with literacy and numeracy difficulties had struggled at the first stage of their formal education. They tended to perform poorly in the tests at 7 and by the time they were 11, when they were tested again, the gap between their performance and that of their peers without skills difficulties was wider.

Although more of those with poor basic skills were assessed as needing special help when they were at school, substantial proportions had not received any. Parents of those with poor skills were rated by teachers as less interested in their children's educational progress than those with good skills. When they were 16, more of those who had difficulties as adults were assessed with a behavioural disorder on the Rutter scale (Rutter et al, 1970) and truanting was common. Although the vast majority of all cohort members (93%) attended a local authority funded secondary school, the composition of the comprehensive and secondary modern schools they did attend was heavily biased towards manual family intakes and against high numbers taking public examinations at 16. Similarly, cohort members with poor adult literacy and numeracy tended to have been located in the non-examination school streams.

- As early as age 7, men and women with very low skills at 37 had the lowest average reading and maths scores. By 11, men with very low literacy in adulthood scored half that of men with good literacy in the reading test; in the maths test, the average 11 year score of men with very low numeracy was one third that of men with good numeracy.

- 40% of adults with very low literacy or very low numeracy were thought not to have had (respectively) reading or maths difficulties by their teachers at age 7, compared with 80% of those with good literacy or 88% with good numeracy.

- In the opinion of teachers, 26% of those with very low literacy as adults needed additional help at age 7 but did not get it, 12% received help and 2% attended a special school.

- More parents of adults with very low literacy (29% mothers, 32% fathers) or very low numeracy (19% mothers, 21% fathers) were rated by teachers as showing 'little interest' in their education when they were 7. By age 16, 39% of mothers and 48% of fathers of adults with very low literacy were rated by teachers as showing 'little interest' in their education. In contrast, just under 7% of mothers or fathers of cohort members with good literacy were rated as showing little interest at either ages 7 or 16.

- 64% of men and 71% of women with very low literacy truanted from school at age 16. This compared with 47% of men and 43% of women with good literacy.

- No adults with very low literacy and just 4% with very low numeracy had been to a grammar or independent school, compared with 33% of adults with good literacy or numeracy.

Transition from School to Work

Disadvantaged by their poor educational achievements, many more of the men and women with poor basic skills left school at the earliest opportunity, and the great majority still had no formal qualifications at 23. When they were 11 most boys with poor basic skills had aspirations to work in manual occupations, though 'sportsman' was also popular. The most popular occupational choices for girls with poor skills were in the 'personal services', or being 'at home' full-time. In reality, unskilled or semi-skilled low grade work was the common destination for many of these early school leavers lacking basic skills. Few received even basic *'on the job'* training and many more experienced long term unemployment, redundancy and being sacked.

- Among early school leavers, 52% of men and 75% of women with very low literacy had not entered into apprenticeships – the quality training of the mid-1970s – compared with 11% of men and 45% of women with good literacy.

- Twice as many men with very low literacy or numeracy had been made redundant or sacked from their first job compared with their counterparts who had good skills (30% to 15% literacy; 27% to 14% numeracy).

- Between 16 and 23, men with very low literacy or numeracy were four times as likely to have experienced two or more years of unemployment as men who had good literacy or any other level of numeracy (12% to 3% literacy, 11% to 3% numeracy). Women with very low literacy were three times as likely to have been unemployed for one year or more compared with women who had good numeracy (18% to 5%).

Adult Working Life

By age 33, although some men and women with poor skills had managed to gain qualifications, those with very low literacy were still by far the most likely to have no qualifications. Differences in labour market experiences remained very apparent between skills groups. More women with poor skills took on long term home-care responsibilities, while poorly skilled men experienced long term unemployment. For those who had ever been employed between age 23 and 33, men and women with poor literacy and numeracy were again unlikely to have received any work-related training. For those that did, the quality was of a much lower standard. Women who had ever worked fared less well than men, but those with poor skills fared the worst.

- Women with very low literacy or very low numeracy were at least three times as likely to have never held a full-time job between 23 and 33, as women with good skills (55% to 15% literacy, 38% to 12% numeracy). Just 14% of women with very low numeracy had been in continuous full-time employment during this time, as compared with 33% of women with good numeracy.

- 5 times as many men with very low literacy or numeracy had not held a full-time job between 23 and 33 as men who had good skills (18% to 4% literacy, 16% to 3% numeracy). During the same time, 7% of men with very low numeracy had been unemployed for five or more years, compared with less than 1% of men with good numeracy.

- 66% of men with very low literacy and 59% of men with very low numeracy had not received any work-related training from an employer. By contrast, 36% of men with good literacy and 31% with good numeracy had not received training; those with training had usually attended at least two 3-day training courses.

Most important influences on adult basic skills

By building up a picture of conditions and experiences at home, school and work it was possible to see how much of the variation in literacy and numeracy scores could be accounted for in terms of earlier experiences, and which early life factors contributed most to the explanation. The statistical technique of multiple regression, applied separately for men and women, enabled us to build up a picture of the sequences of experiences and influences which formed the contexts in which problems with basic skills emerged.

Initially, factors present at birth were used to predict literacy and numeracy scores at age 37; information from age 7, 11, 16, 23 and 33 was then incorporated in sequence. For both sexes, numeracy was the more sensitive outcome measure, with a higher percentage of variation (over 40%) in the scores being explained by childhood circumstances and experiences at earlier ages. Numeracy had closer direct links with early cognitive skills than literacy. Adult basic skills in men appeared to have more direct ties with early cognitive ability, than was the case for women. In contrast, women's basic skills appeared to be influenced by a broader set of experiences and circumstances.

At birth

Factors present at birth could explain some of the variation in literacy or numeracy performance at 37 – in the order of 6%. The higher the social class at birth the better the adult literacy and numeracy score for both men and women. Their mother's age at leaving full-time education was a particularly strong predictor of literacy and numeracy for men.

Up to 7

The overall variation explained in adult basic skills quadrupled. For both men and women the strongest individual predictors were cognitive test results, together with parental interest. Being read to as a child and school attendance were additional predictors of a good performance for women, whereas family disadvantage (overcrowding in the home) predicted a poor performance for men.

Up to 11

The strength of the overall relationship between circumstances and experiences up to age 11 and adult basic skills continued to increase, with a more diverse set of experiences helping explain performance differences for women. Reading performance and copying design skills at 7, both cognitive tests at 11 and family disadvantage (free school meals at 11) strongly predicted adult literacy for both men and women. Maths performance at 7 was additionally important for men, while for women, the interest and support of parents and school attendance at 7 predicted later literacy. For adult numeracy, maths performance at 11 was the only significant predictor common to men and women. Early cognitive tests, parental support and interest were all predictors of a good performance for women, family disadvantage (free school meals) predicted *poor* skills. For men, maths score, copying design skills and school attendance at 7 all predicted good numeracy, whereas another indicator of difficult family circumstances, overcrowding in the home at 7, predicted *poor* numeracy.

Up to 16

The percentage of variation explained in adult literacy and numeracy continued to rise, but more slowly. For both men and women the strongest predictors of literacy were reading test scores at 16. Maths performance at 11 was the strongest predictor of adult numeracy. For women, reading skills at 7 and public examination results at 16 independently predicted literacy and numeracy performance. For men, maths ability and copying design skills at 7 predicted performance in both adult tests. Indicators of parental interest/educational support predicted good adult literacy. For women, parental interest/support (at 7 and 16) and early school attendance were particularly important, while disruptive behaviour at 16 (Rutter et al, 1970) was linked with *poor* performance. For men, parental interest and going to a middle class school (percent of fathers in a non-manual occupation at their secondary school) predicted good literacy; overcrowding in the home at 7 remained a predictor of *poor* skills. Factors predicting *poor* adult numeracy for men included poor school attendance and overcrowded housing, and for women, being read to as a child predicted *good* literacy.

Up to 23

The percentage of variation explained in adult test performance continued to increase slightly. Highest qualification held at 23 and reading test performance at 16 were the strongest predictors of adult basic skills for both men and women. Of the new explanatory variables introduced, work-related training predicted literacy and numeracy for men, but only numeracy for women. Months spent in full-time employment (age 16-23) predicted good literacy in women; months unemployed during the same period predicted *poor* numeracy for men.

Early cognitive performance maintained its independent relationship with adult literacy. Reading and copying design test scores predicted good skills for men and women. Family disadvantage (free school meals) continued to predict *poor* basic skills. For women, parental support factors throughout childhood, school attendance (at 7) and single-sex secondary education predicted good literacy. Disruptive school behaviour (at 16) predicted *poor* skills. For men, predictors of good literacy were parental interest (at 16) and the percentage of fathers in a non-manual occupation at their secondary school.

Maths performance at 11 was a strong predictor of adult numeracy for both men and women. Maths performance and public examination results at 16 also predicted numeracy for women; family disadvantage (free school meals) predicted *poor* numeracy. For men the 'draw-a-man' test score at 7 predicted good skills; overcrowding in the home at 7 and disruptive school behaviour at 16 both predicted *poor* adult numeracy.

Up to 33

Even at this stage, an additional one or two percent of the variance in basic skills could be explained. Qualifications and labour market experiences gained between 23 and 33 were significant predictors of adult basic skills. Months spent in full-time employment from 23 predicted literacy of men and women, and numeracy of men. Earlier training and youth unemployment (16 to 23) remained key factors for men's numeracy, and highest qualification held at 33 replaced the highest qualification variable at 23. For women, public examination results at 16 predicted their literacy and numeracy; highest qualification at 23 predicted literacy, work-related training predicted numeracy. With respect to the early childhood variables, a near identical set of significant predictors of adult literacy and numeracy ability were present at 33 as were present at 23.

Conclusions

Early cognitive performance variables are the dominant predictors of later reading and maths skills in childhood, and adult literacy and numeracy. Much of the influence of family disadvantage, parental support and schooling is mediated by cognitive attainments in schooling. However, some childhood experiences retain an independent influence on adult skills including measures of family disadvantage (free school meals, overcrowded living conditions), parental interest and support (being read to as a child, parent-teacher meetings). The cognitive success of women is related to a broader set of conditions and experiences than for men, but measures of family disadvantage and parental support are important for both. The kind of secondary education entered is also important, as indicated by single-sex education for women, and a high percentage of fathers at their school in non-manual occupations for men. School attendance at an early age is also a positive influence for women.

Experiences post-16 are more complex, both arising from and reinforcing the basic skills. Highest qualifications held at 23 or 33 are important predictors, but also reflect earlier education experiences. Months in full-time employment are more important for men, particularly after 23. However, this was the time of the 1980s economic recession when those with poor skills were most likely to be pushed out of the labour market. In these circumstances there is likely to be less opportunity to strengthen basic skills; they are more likely to deteriorate. Early unemployment appears particularly detrimental for men's numeracy. On the other hand, work-related training appears to enhance literacy and numeracy for men, and numeracy for women.

The kind of vicious circle revealed can be seen as an accelerating process beginning early in life and speeding up as children move through education and on to work. Those who fall behind at school, subsequently miss out early on in the labour market and this further reduces their chances of catching up on the basic skills. Unemployment reduces their opportunities further. As a result it becomes more difficult to get back on the employment track. Set against this negative cycle is the positive one identified with the prospect of improvement when opportunities are present. Through training and a wide range of the every day functions of modern employment, basic skills are both called upon and practised. This contrasts with the deterioration that unemployment brings.

The conclusion to draw is that at every stage in life educational intervention to enhance basic skills has relevance and can be effective. In early life home-school links serve as the critical buffer to support learning and to prevent slippage in their acquisition. Later on in school and at work, wherever written or numerical applications are in use, there are opportunities to improve basic skills. Targeted intervention capitalises on these to add an educational component to every task in working life.

CHAPTER 1

Background and Methods

Introduction

Success in adult life is becoming increasingly dependent on attaining school qualifications, and building upon them, through further education and training, to obtain the diverse range of skills demanded by modern employment. The idea of a learning society (Hussein, 1989; Coffield, 1997) underlines the point that accelerating technological change transforms the nature of occupations and employment. This means that school and work need to become increasingly interwoven, with education, training and employment, following each other in circular order rather than in the single linear sequence of the past. Many commentators have noted Britain's slow start in adapting to the new circumstances, compared with our main competitors (e.g. Green and Steedman, 1997). But employment is only one area of adult life where 'education counts'. The increasing complexity of modern living, the development of such channels of communication as the Internet, the regulations that need to be understood, and the forms that have to be filled in, create increasing difficulty for those without basic education (Carey, Low and Hansbro, 1997; Lacroix and Tremblay, 1997). Poor qualifications and skills lie at the heart of what is increasingly described as 'social exclusion': the inability of a minority of individuals to engage with, and participate fully in, occupational and community life.

Underpinning the difficulties these individuals have is 'typically' a weak grasp of the basic skills of literacy and numeracy. Employers' expectations have been rising steadily about the proficiency in these skills that potential employees are expected to have (Industry in Education, 1997). To solve the problems of those individuals who, after eleven years of schooling, still have difficulty reading and calculating, we need to be able to identify the ages and stages earlier in life when they begin to fall behind.

The opportunity to carry out such an investigation comes from the unique research resources we have in Britain in the birth cohort studies. These are national longitudinal enquiries, based on following up single samples of people from birth into adulthood. The National Child Development Study (NCDS) has collected data on over 17,000 people born in a single week in 1958, and subsequently at ages 7, 11, 16, 23, 33 and 37 (10% sample). The 1970 British Cohort Study (BCS70), similarly began with a sample of over 17,000 people born in a single week in 1970, who have been followed-up in subsequent surveys at ages 5, 10, 16, 21 (10% sample) and most recently at 26. A series of studies using these data sets has been carried out for the Basic Skills Agency (BSA), analysing the effects of poor basic skills on adult life (Ekinsmyth and Bynner, 1994; Bynner and Parsons 1997a & b), and using the BCS70 longitudinal data from 21 back to birth to identify the origins of cohort members' difficulties (Bynner and Steedman, 1995). In each case 10% samples of the original birth cohort were used. The present research draws on the 10% sample of the NCDS cohort to trace the varying circumstances and influences on the development and deterioration of basic skills from birth to 37.

The earlier BCS70 study showed that poor basic skills in adulthood were often associated with a cycle of deprivation in childhood in which the child's family and school life became increasingly out of step. Adverse family circumstances and the poor educational experiences of parents impeded the children's ability to take advantage of what they were being taught at school, setting them off on a train of poor achievement, which they in turn were likely to pass on to their own children. The key conclusion for policy from the study was the importance of early intervention involving parents and teachers of the kind that the Basic Skills Agency's family literacy programme represents. The study also reinforced the value of later intervention, demonstrating that despite the predictability of adult basic skills problems from early experience at home and at school, there was sufficient fluidity in their acquisition to give value to remediation right into adult life.

This new study using the 10% sample of the NCDS cohort at age 37, offers an opportunity to test, replicate and expand the findings about the antecedents of basic skills problems in the BCS70 cohort over a much longer time span. At the time of the BCS70 survey, many of the 21 year olds were still involved in higher education. The relationship of skills acquisition and preservation with experiences of further education, employment and training could not be fully explored. With the NCDS survey at 37 we can examine these relationships from birth through to adult life. We know that adults with poor skills have restricted access to employment opportunities. We also know that these negative labour market experiences have far reaching social, economic and psychological consequences for the individual. Do they also have a detrimental effect on an individual's basic skills?

Assessment of Literacy and Numeracy

Each cohort member was interviewed about their work, family life, health and well-being at 37. At the end of the interview, functional literacy and numeracy assessments, designed by the National Foundation for Educational Research, were completed. There were eight literacy tasks and nine numeracy tasks, each of which consisted of a visual stimulus, such as a page from 'yellow pages' (literacy), or items to purchase in a shop (numeracy), and a number of questions to be answered about it or exercises to be performed. The tasks were grouped at different levels corresponding to the BSA Wordpower and Numberpower standards with a reasonable spread of tasks at each level (Appendix 1 gives examples of the questions and explains the scoring method).

Of the 2144 cohort members originally selected for the survey, 1714 took part in the interview – a response rate of 79%. 1711 completed satisfactory literacy assessments and 1702 satisfactory numeracy assessments.

The literacy assessment yielded a maximum score of 23 and the numeracy assessment a maximum score of 18. The literacy scores were highly skewed towards high scores, i.e., most people could do most of the tasks. The numeracy scores were much more evenly distributed, reflecting the much higher prevalence of numeracy difficulties.

For the purposes of comparing the characteristics of people at different levels of literacy and numeracy, cohort members were classified into four literacy and numeracy groups, 'very low', 'low', 'average' and 'good'. The cutting points reflected the more widespread difficulties with numeracy than literacy and natural breaks in the distributions of the scores. Six percent had very low literacy skills, 13% had low literacy skills, 38% had average skills and 43% had good skills. The comparable percentages for numeracy were 23% very low, 25% low, 25% average and 27% good. (Fuller details are given in Bynner and Parsons, 1997a).

The report

This study looks behind the problems of men and women with poor basic skills reported in *It Doesn't Get Any Better* (Bynner and Parsons, 1997a). It points to the kinds of interventions, at the different stages in life, that are most likely to succeed in helping people to master the basic skills. Possible influences on basic skills arising from circumstances and experiences in different life domains are examined individually under headings describing the areas and stages of life in which they occur: Family and Home Circumstances; Early Education and Schooling; Transition from School to Work, Adult Working Life. We then use multivariate statistical analysis to see how powerful all the influences taken together are in explaining literacy and numeracy performance at age 37, and to find out which of them are the most critical.

As basic skills difficulties can have a quite different impact on the course of men and women's lives (Bynner, Morphy and Parsons, 1997), this analysis, unlike the previous study, was carried out separately for men and women. Throughout the report the results are generally presented by gender. Overall, the analysis confirms our earlier conclusions that the origins of basic skills difficulties lie principally in early childhood and reflect the breakdown in the relationship between school and home. Reasons for the breakdown lie in material deprivation typically suffered by these families and the parents' inability, based often on their own poor educational attainment, to provide the learning reinforcement at home that teachers tend to take for granted. Later on, through adolescence and early adulthood, the research points to a number of factors that can help to mitigate these adverse early education effects. These provide the basis for targeted basic skills educational interventions at school, at home and in the work place.

CHAPTER 2

Family and Home Circumstances

Introduction

Of all the factors impinging on young children's educational potential, the material circumstances of family life are probably the most crucial. This is not to say that families cannot rise above their economic disadvantages to provide the educational support that young children need, but that such conditions are often accompanied by a set of adverse factors, working against the child's full cognitive development. Poor home conditions, such as overcrowding, can restrict opportunities for early learning. Often the young parents who live in them are themselves disadvantaged educationally. They may not know how to give their children the educational preparation that lies at the foundations of primary school education. In 1958, when the NCDS cohort were born, the compensation for this absence of support, provided by nursery education, was a very rare option. Most of the cohort members who grew up in poor physical conditions were looked after by parents or child-minders before they went to school.

Parental education

Parents' educational level is strongly related to the educational attainments of their children. In our earlier BCS70 study, mothers of those with basic skills difficulties were much more likely to have left school at 15 or younger, and a far higher percentage of either parent was without formal qualifications (Bynner and Steedman, 1995).

NCDS cohort members were born in 1958. At that time, in the order of 70% of people left school at the minimum age of 16 and entry to higher education was under 10%. Overall, 58% of cohort members' fathers and 46% of their mothers had left full-time education before their fifteenth birthday; just 8% of fathers and 6% of mothers had remained in education post-18. As expected, differences in the educational experiences of cohort members' parents were very strongly related to the cohort members' adult literacy and numeracy.

Figure 2.1 shows the percentages of cohort members whose parents had stayed on at school beyond the age of 16, for each of the four 37 year literacy and numeracy categories. Post-16 education had been experienced by no more than 13% of mothers or fathers of cohort members with either very low or low literacy, or very low numeracy. In contrast, this level of education had been experienced by at least 30% (highest at 37%) of the parents of cohort members with good literacy or numeracy. (A measure of highest qualification held by a parent was not available).

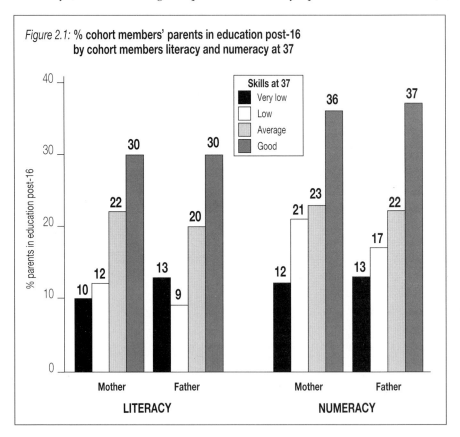

Figure 2.1: % cohort members' parents in education post-16 by cohort members literacy and numeracy at 37

Social class

Two percent of all cohort members were born to single mothers, seven percent of those with very low literacy skills at 37. For all others, social class was derived from the occupation of the male head of household at the time of their birth. In 1958 the labour market was such that the majority of jobs were *manual*. Just 29% of all the cohort members' fathers were in *non*-manual occupations at this time. This dropped to 14% for fathers of those with very low literacy or very low numeracy, and rose to 40% for the fathers of cohort members with good numeracy (40%). Sixteen years later, 39% of all fathers held non-manual positions, but differences related to cohort members' own skills were almost as pronounced. Less than 25% of those with very low literacy or numeracy had fathers in non-manual occupations, as compared with 50% of those with good literacy or numeracy.

Financial difficulties

Direct and indirect evidence of financial difficulties during childhood was more evident for those with poor basic skills. When cohort members were age 7, parents of those with very low literacy or numeracy were around *five* times as likely to report experiencing financial hardship as parents of those cohort members with good literacy or numeracy (19% to 4% literacy, 12% to 2% numeracy). These differences had dropped to no more than three times as likely at age 11, which was the boom time during the late 1960s. However, the more objective measure of financial hardship, that of children receiving free school meals, revealed telling differences between the basic skills groups. At age 11, just 8% of all cohort members received free school meals. From Figure 2.2 we can see that adults with

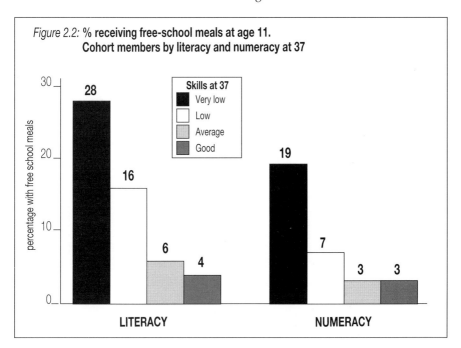

Figure 2.2: % receiving free-school meals at age 11.
Cohort members by literacy and numeracy at 37

very low literacy were seven times more likely to have received free school meals at 11 when compared with adults who had good literacy (28% to 4%). Adults with very low numeracy were six times as likely to receive free school meals compared with those with good numeracy (19% to 3%).

Housing and overcrowding in the home

At age 7, 47% of all cohort members lived in owner-occupied accommodation, 35% rented from their local council and 12% rented privately. By age 16, 58% of the cohort lived in owner-occupied housing; 33% were in council accommodation and just 5% were now in rented housing from a private source. Those most likely to have lived in council accommodation were cohort members with very low literacy or numeracy; the least likely were cohort members with good literacy or numeracy. Figure 2.3 shows that over half of those with very low literacy lived in

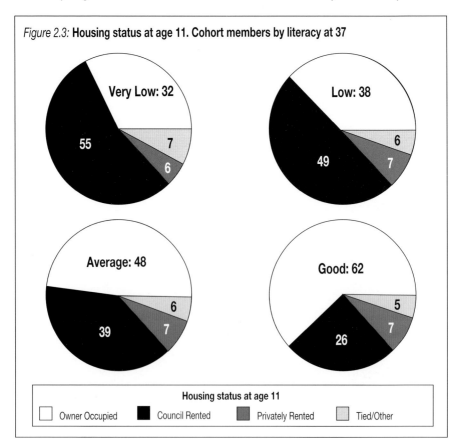

Figure 2.3: **Housing status at age 11. Cohort members by literacy at 37**

Very Low: 32

55   7   6

Low: 38

49   6   7

Average: 48

39   6   7

Good: 62

26   5   7

Housing status at age 11

☐ Owner Occupied   ■ Council Rented   ▨ Privately Rented   ▨ Tied/Other accommodation rented from their council when they were 11, compared with one quarter of cohort members who had good literacy (55% to 26%). Much the same degree of difference was found for numeracy.

The Office for National Statistics defines over-crowded accommodation as a home where there is 'more than 1 person per room'. Such conditions were experienced by more than half of all cohort members when age 7, 11 or 16. Although differences between the basic skills groups with respect to overcrowding diminished slightly over time, reflecting general improvements in housing quality, at every age the highest proportions living in over-crowded conditions were the cohort members with the poorest skills.

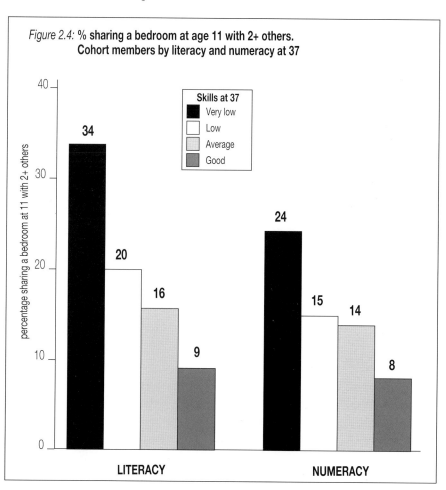

Figure 2.4: % sharing a bedroom at age 11 with 2+ others.
Cohort members by literacy and numeracy at 37

An even sharper indicator of over-crowded childhood living conditions is the number of cohort members who actually shared a bedroom. This again declined as cohort members got older, reflecting both a rise in the families' overall standard of living and older siblings moving out. At age 7, two-thirds of those with very low literacy or numeracy shared a bedroom in comparison with just under half of those with good literacy or numeracy. But as Figure 2.4 shows, when we move up the overcrowding scale the difference becomes even larger. 34% of cohort members with very low literacy shared a bedroom with at least two others at age 11, as did 24% of those with very low numeracy skills. This compared with less than 10% of those in the group with good literacy or numeracy skills. At 16, around half of those with very low literacy or very low numeracy still shared a bedroom, as opposed to less than a third of those with good literacy or good numeracy (48% to 28% literacy, 46% to 30% numeracy).

Lifestyle

During the interview at 37, cohort members were asked whether they remembered newspapers, books, a radio, television, telephone, etc, being in their family home between the ages of 11 and 16. Most members of all literacy and numeracy groups reported having a daily or weekly newspaper, comics, a dictionary, a radio and a television. However, as Figure 2.5 shows, magazines, 25+ books, an encyclopaedia and a telephone were far less likely to have been in the childhood home of adults with poor basic skills. Those least likely to have had these items in their homes were adults with very low literacy.

To check the accuracy of these recollections, we looked back at information collected at age 11 and found, as reported in adulthood, that 87% of all cohort members said they watched TV most days, and 52% read either a newspaper, magazine or comic most days. In contrast, whereas over half of adults with good literacy (53%) or good numeracy (55%) read a book outside of school most days at 11, this dropped to around one-third of adults with very low literacy (32%) or very low numeracy (38%). These differences reflect the relative lack of books in the family homes of the cohort members with poor basic skills. Similar differences were found with respect to 'going often' to the local library, where those with good skills were the most likely to go.

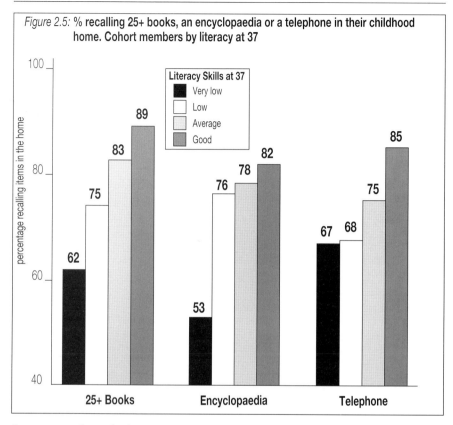

Figure 2.5: % recalling 25+ books, an encyclopaedia or a telephone in their childhood home. Cohort members by literacy at 37

Summary and conclusions

Poverty and disadvantaged circumstances were more evident in the childhood of the adults with basic skills difficulties and their parents were the least likely to have experienced post-16 education. Books were also less common in their homes when they were children.

- Adults with very low literacy skills were seven times more likely to have received free school meals at age 11 than adults who had good literacy skills (28% to 4%); adults with very low numeracy skills were six times as likely to have received free school meals as those with good numeracy skills (19% to 3%).

- Adults with very low literacy or very low numeracy skills were twice as likely to have grown up in Council rented accommodation as adults who had good skills (55% to 26% by literacy), and were at least three times as likely to share their bedroom with 2+ other family members at age 11 (34% to 9% by literacy; 24% to 8% by numeracy).

- No more than 1 in 8 mothers or fathers of cohort members with either very low literacy (10% mothers, 13% fathers) or very low numeracy skills (12% mothers, 13% fathers) had participated in post-16 education. By contrast 1 in 3 parents of cohort members with good skills (30% mothers and fathers for literacy; 36% mothers, 37% fathers for numeracy) had participated in post school education.

CHAPTER 3

Early Education and Schooling

Introduction

We have seen from the previous chapter that the material conditions of early childhood are strongly related to basic skills problems in adulthood. These are of course not direct causes of failure to learn. As we noted they represent more a set of interacting circumstances in which the necessary preparations for early education are absent. At the core of this preparation is constructive play with children. In the earlier BCS70 survey (Bynner and Steedman, 1995), those children who up to the age of 5 had developed the best visual motor skills, as revealed through a 'draw-a-man' test, maintained their advantage over the others right through to adulthood. Such skills are very much the product of interactions between adults and children, either in effective nursery/kindergarten provision, or at home.

Educated parents place great emphasis on using play with children to improve their learning, using their own understanding of the education process and their own early childhood experience, to underpin their role as early educators. They tend to read to their children at an early age and use every opportunity to enhance their children's cognitive skills. Parents without these attributes may not have such implicit educational understanding. Nor, under the very difficult conditions in which many of them live, do they have the personal resources or even the will to help their children learn effectively. The television set frequently provides the main means by which the children are kept occupied. Such projects as 'Sesame Street' were designed precisely to try to turn the television experience into something with educational value. The broader strategy recognised through the Basic Skills Agency's family literacy programme focuses on helping parents to help their children learn to read. By tapping into the motivation that the great majority of parents have to see their children succeed, not only are the children helped but the parents' own reading improves as well. This gives further benefits to the children and hence a set of interacting positive influences on the child's learning is built up. In this chapter we examine the kinds of help parents were giving their children with learning to read, and how this related to their literacy and numeracy in adulthood.

Early development and starting school

When they were 7 years old the cohort members' parents were asked about the early development of their children. Just 3% of the cohort had not walked unaided by the time they reached one-and-a-half years old; 6% were not able to talk by age two. 6% had stammered at some time and 8% had experienced some other speech difficulty. In all these development areas, although mothers of cohort members with very low literacy were slightly more likely than the others to report that the child had developed slightly later or had experienced physical difficulties, differences were marginal.

Only 13% of all cohort members had attended either a private or local authority day nursery, in advance of primary school, which generally started on a full-time basis between age four-and-a-half and five years. Over 80% of all parents said their child had settled into school within the first month, and there were no

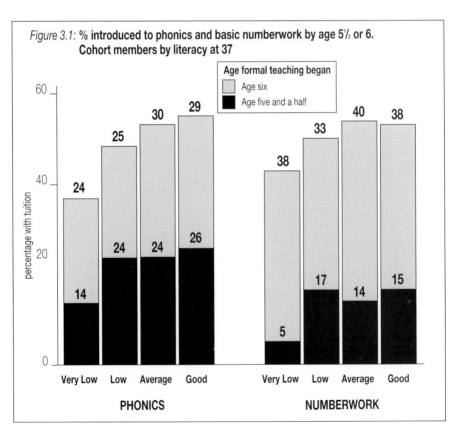

Figure 3.1: % **introduced to phonics and basic numberwork by age 5½ or 6. Cohort members by literacy at 37**

noticeable differences with respect to these experiences between the basic skills groups. However, according to their teachers, having experience of teaching of phonics and basic numberwork before age 7 did differ somewhat across groups. Figure 3.1 shows that over half of all cohort members had been initially introduced to phonics and basic numberwork by age six. But in comparison with other groups, adults with very low literacy at 37 were far less likely to have begun their tuition by age 5½: 14% had started basic phonic teaching by this age compared with 26% of those with good literacy skills. (17% of those with very low literacy had teachers who did not know when their phonics tuition had started compared with 12% overall). There were barely any differences between numeracy groups with respect to these early learning experiences.

Early parental support

Cohort members with poor basic skills were also less likely to have been read to as a child. During a typical week at age 7, just 35% of mothers of those with very low literacy (in adulthood) and 39% of those with very low numeracy had read to their child. This compared with over half (52%) of mothers of children who as adults demonstrated good literacy or numeracy. Fathers were less likely, overall, than mothers to have read to their children. Those who had very low literacy at 37 were again the least likely to have been read to by their fathers. Just 19% had this experience, compared with around one in three (32% to 38%) of those in all other basic skills groups.

The importance of being read to from a very early age is well documented (e.g., Bynner and Steedman, 1995), as is the influence of adult role models. Reading for interest was reported by fewer parents of adults with poor basic skills. When the cohort was age 7, 60% of mothers and 48% of fathers of adults with very low literacy reported 'hardly ever' reading a book; likewise 53% of mothers and 40% of fathers of adults with very low numeracy. In contrast, for adults with good literacy or numeracy, around one in three mothers (35% literacy, 34% numeracy) and less than one in four fathers (22% literacy, 21% numeracy) reported 'hardly ever' reading a book.

Those with very low skills as adults were also most likely to have had a father who left the overall management of their child to the mother: 1 in 5 (20%) of those with very low literacy and 1 in 7 (14%) with very low numeracy had a father who had totally 'left it to mum' in comparison with 1 in 14 (7%) of those with good literacy or numeracy.

Early cognitive performance

In each of the surveys at 7, 11 and 16, cohort members had taken various cognitive ability tests. Reading and numberwork were assessed at all three ages, visual motor skills at 7 (see Appendix 2 for details of all tests). Reading and numberwork provide the foundations on which other skills are continuously built and developed. They need to be in place from an early age.

By examining the results of the first tests of the early cognitive ability of NCDS members at 7, at least one year after formal teaching had begun, it was possible to see if adults with literacy and numeracy difficulties had struggled at the first stage of their formal education. If these basic skills were found to be absent at 7, teachers and parents would know immediately that children showing clear signs of difficulties would need additional support if they were to keep in step with the rest of their class.

For easy comparison, we re-scaled all school test scores to fall within the range 0-10. Table 3.1a gives the mean (average) scores obtained in the reading tests at age 7, 11 and 16 for men and women compared across the adult literacy groups. Table 3.1b gives the mean scores in the maths tests at age 7, 11 and 16 for men and women compared across the adult numeracy groups. The 'standard deviations' which are also shown in the tables give a measure of the variation of the scores around the mean.

As early as age 7, men and women with very low basic skills at 37 had the *lowest* mean reading and maths scores; men and women with good basic skills at 37 had the *highest* mean scores. These differences got larger at the older ages of 11 and 16. As literacy to some extent underpins the acquisition of basic numeracy, it is not surprising that adults with very low literacy also had the lowest mean scores in the maths tests at all three age points.

Thus at age 7 the mean reading test score for men with good literacy was 1.7 times higher than that of men with very low literacy (8.4 to 4.9). By age 11 those with good adult literacy had a mean score which was exactly *twice* the mean score of

Table 3.1a: *Mean Scores attained in Reading Tests during Childhood – Men and Women by Literacy at 37*

	Reading Tests								
	Age 7			Age 11			Age 16		
	Mean	sd	N	Mean	sd	N	Mean	sd	N
Men									
Very Low	4.9	2.7	34	2.8	1.9	28	4.4	2.7	32
Low	6.2	2.7	78	3.6	1.4	70	6.2	1.8	59
Average	7.6	2.2	266	4.5	1.6	262	7.3	1.8	216
Good	8.4	1.9	334	5.6	1.7	326	8.4	1.3	292
Women									
Very Low	6.1	2.7	51	3.0	1.6	53	4.5	2.3	38
Low	7.4	2.4	126	4.0	1.4	109	6.3	1.7	102
Average	8.4	2.0	316	4.8	1.5	302	7.6	1.5	272
Good	8.9	1.5	321	5.7	1.5	311	8.3	1.1	275
Max Score	10			10			10		

Table 3.1b: *Mean Scores attained in Maths Tests during Childhood – Men and Women by Literacy at 37*

	Reading Tests								
	Age 7			Age 11			Age 16		
	Mean	sd	N	Mean	sd	N	Mean	sd	N
Men									
Very Low	4.0	2.4	128	2.1	1.8	120	2.7	1.7	108
Low	4.8	2.1	163	3.5	2.1	153	3.7	1.7	126
Average	5.6	2.3	175	4.5	2.2	174	4.9	2.0	144
Good	6.6	2.3	241	6.2	2.2	238	6.3	2.0	220
Women									
Very Low	4.1	2.3	206	2.3	1.7	200	2.5	1.4	177
Low	4.9	2.2	224	4.0	1.9	212	3.8	1.6	188
Average	5.9	2.3	201	5.1	2.2	195	4.9	2.0	170
Good	6.4	2.2	172	6.5	2.0	160	6.1	2.1	145
Max Score	10			10			10		

men with very low skills (5.6 to 2.8). For maths the ratio moved from 1.7 at age 7 to *three* at age 11 (6.2 to 2.1). For women, the widening of the gap between age 7 and 11 for those with good or very low literacy was slightly smaller, changing from 1.5 times higher (8.9 to 6.1) to 1.9 times higher (5.7 to 3.0) for reading test scores and 1.6 times higher (6.4 to 4.1) to 2.8 times higher (6.5 to 2.3) for maths scores. At age 16, the differences in the mean test scores were retained at much the same level, suggesting that the critical problems in acquiring both literacy and numeracy arise in primary school. Difficulties can clearly be overcome later on in life, but the optimum time for ensuring that they never occur is in the early years of primary school.

These connections between basic skills problems in adulthood and poor cognitive skills while at school are usefully summarised by correlation coefficients. These have a range of –1 to +1. A coefficient of +1 means that scores on the school test perfectly predict scores on the adult test. A coefficient of –1 indicates that the scores are similarly perfectly related but in the opposite direction, i.e. high scores on the school test are associated with low scores on the adult test and so on. A correlation coefficient close to 0 indicates little or no (linear) relationship between the scores.

Table 3.2 shows the correlation coefficients for scores in these cognitive tests taken at 7, 11 and 16 with those obtained in the adult literacy and numeracy assessment. Correlations between reading test scores and adult literacy and numeracy scores increased strikingly with age. A correlation of .37 was recorded at age 7 for reading with literacy and numeracy, and at age 16 correlations reached .58 with literacy, and .56 with numeracy. The correlations between maths test scores and adult literacy and numeracy scores showed slightly different patterns with substantial increases occurring between ages 7 and 11, and much smaller ones between 11 and 16. The two motor co-ordination tests at 7 ('draw-a-man' and copying design test) had lower correlations than the reading and maths tests at the same age. The correlations between public examination scores at 16 and adult literacy and numeracy scores were also at a lower level than the correlations for the reading and maths test scores at that age.

Table 3.2: *Correlations of childhood cognitive test scores and adult literacy and numeracy scores at 37*

	Literacy score at 37	Numeracy score at 37
At Age 7		
Copying Design Test	.25	.24
Draw-a-Man	.22	.24
Reading	.37	.37
Maths	.31	.37
At Age 11		
Reading	.45	.47
Maths	.45	.56
At age 16		
Reading	.58	.56
Maths	.46	.57
Exam score	.38	.45

Recognition of and help provided for early cognitive difficulties

Early identification of basic skills difficulties, together with early help and assistance from both teachers and parents, may be critical in the child's acquisition of the basic skills. This is because difficulties *if not detected* are compounded over time.

In the schools cohort members attended, form teachers were asked whether or not they thought the cohort member, then a child, needed any additional help or special education at that time or was likely to need it at some time in the future. At age 7, 88% of all cohort members were thought not to need any additional help at school, 7% did not receive help but teachers believed it would have been of benefit, 5% did receive help and 1% attended a special needs school. Differences were striking between adult basic skills groups, particularly for literacy. Figure 3.2 shows that, 60% of adults with very low literacy were thought not to need any help or special education. For 26% some kind of additional help should have been received, but none was (as for 14% of cohort members with very low numeracy), 12% received additional help in their current school and 2% attended a special needs school. For those with good basic skills, over 90% (93% literacy, 94% numeracy) were thought not to need any additional help, 3% of those with good literacy and 2% with good numeracy did not receive the additional help which was thought necessary, 3% received additional help and 1% attended a special needs school.

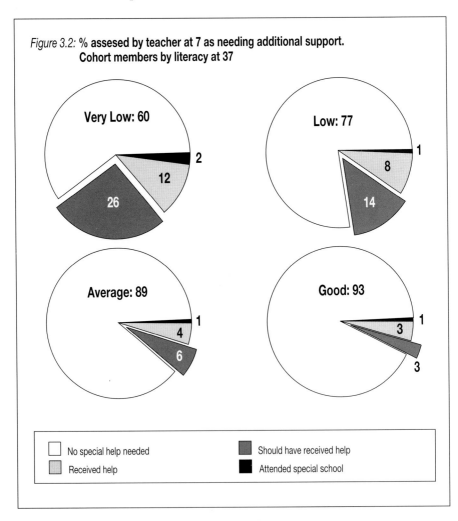

Figure 3.2: **% assesed by teacher at 7 as needing additional support. Cohort members by literacy at 37**

So, did teachers recognise the *specific* difficulties of those with poor adult basic skills when they were at school? When age 7, 11 and 16, teachers were also asked to rate the cohort members' reading and maths skills. Figures 3.3a and 3.3b clearly show that although teachers were far more likely to have assessed adults with poor literacy and numeracy with difficulties as early as 7, 40% of adults with very low literacy or very low numeracy were *not* thought to have had related reading or numberwork difficulties. Similar figures were recorded at age 11 (46% with very low literacy, 37% very low numeracy). Given that the average reading and maths test scores attained by those with very low literacy or very low numeracy were far lower than for adults with good literacy or good numeracy, it is surprising that relatively few were identified as having difficulties.

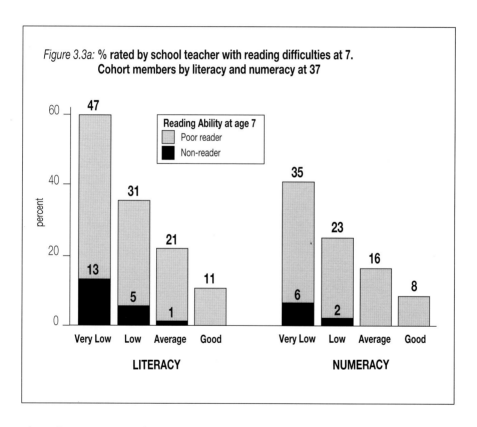

Figure 3.3a: **% rated by school teacher with reading difficulties at 7.
Cohort members by literacy and numeracy at 37**

These figures suggest, first, that basic skill difficulties are often not identified, or if identified not acted upon. Secondly, the figures suggest that the kinds of remedial education provided were inadequate to the task: those who were the target of such help while at school were still likely to have poor basic skills in adulthood. As in previous studies, no correlation appeared between basic skills difficulties and class size.

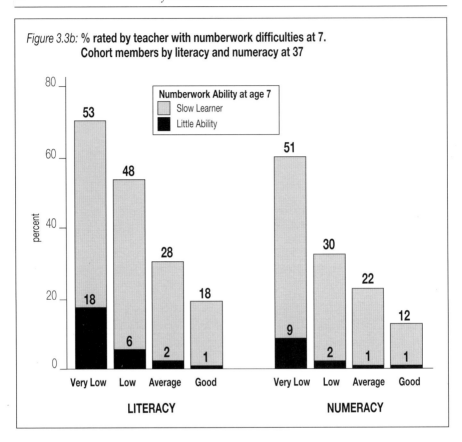

Figure 3.3b: % rated by teacher with numberwork difficulties at 7. Cohort members by literacy and numeracy at 37

School attendance and behaviour

The child's attendance record during a single term at school was recorded by teachers at age 7, 11 and 16. Attendance at school was highest at age 11: 17% had been absent for more than 10% of the term; just 3% for more than one-quarter of the term. Absenteeism at school was notably highest for adults with very low adult literacy. Figure 3.4 shows that in comparison with those who had good literacy, three times as many had missed more than one-quarter of a school term at both 7 (17% to 5%) and 11 (7% to 2%). By age 16 differences were six times as great; 36% to 6%. Differences in school attendance by adult numeracy were not particularly evident until age 16. Although absolute levels of absenteeism were lower, eight times as many adults with very low numeracy missed more than one-quarter of a term of school at age 16 in comparison with adults with good numeracy (24% to 3%).

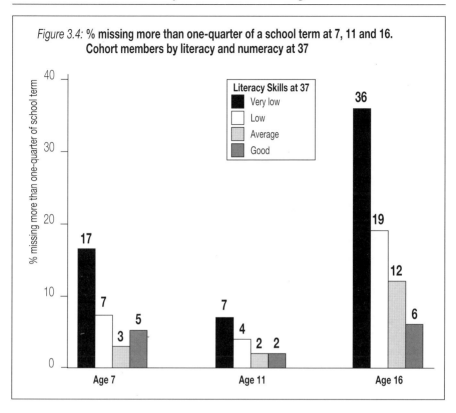

Figure 3.4: **% missing more than one-quarter of a school term at 7, 11 and 16. Cohort members by literacy and numeracy at 37**

At younger ages, much of this absenteeism would have resulted from the various childhood diseases that do the rounds. When cohort members were 11, 4% of all parents reported their child had taken more than one month off school during the preceding year due to health reasons; but this increased threefold to 12% for those with very low literacy. At age 16, 8% of all the cohort had been absent from school for at least one month due to poor health, but the percentage was again much higher for adults with very low literacy – 25% (14% of adults with very low numeracy). At age 16, however, truancy must be considered alongside this question of ill-health. Half of all cohort members reported they had 'truanted' from school in the preceding year. Not surprisingly, truancy was highest for those with poor basic skills. In figure 3.5 we see that 71% of women and 64% of men with very low literacy in adulthood had been absent from school without consent. The lowest level of truancy, 40%, was reported by women with good numeracy. This was also the group who were the least likely to have been absent from school at 16 for one month or more due to health reasons (5%).

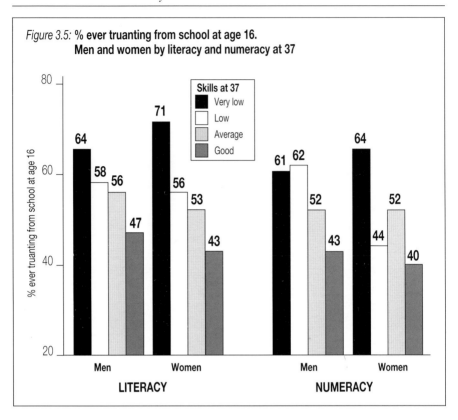

Figure 3.5: % ever truanting from school at age 16.
Men and women by literacy and numeracy at 37

It was not surprising, therefore, to find that men and women with poor skills expressed the least liking for school. At age 16 although 25% of cohort members said they did not like school, this increased to in the order of 40% of those with very low literacy or numeracy – highest at 47% for women with very low literacy. Those with good literacy or numeracy were least likely to state they did not like school.

The education system was clearly not meeting the needs of those who required additional support; by the time the majority were planning their exit from education, few retained any fondness for the institutions where more than a decade had been spent and many were viewed by teachers as disruptive.

Teachers were asked to assess the 'behaviour' of cohort members over the preceding twelve months when they were 16. Twenty-six behaviours, such as 'tends to be on own – rather solitary' or 'bullies other children' make up the Rutter scale (Rutter et al, 1970) and each behaviour is graded as 'doesn't apply (0)' 'applies somewhat (1)' and 'certainly applies (2)' (the full set of behaviours is shown in Appendix 3). A score of nine or more is considered to be representative of a behaviour disorder. Overall, 14% of cohort members (16% men and 13% women) scored 9 or higher. Figure 3.6 shows that differences between adult literacy and numeracy groups on this criterion of problem behaviour were substantial. Teachers gave a score of 9+ to 50% of men and 45% of women with very low literacy.

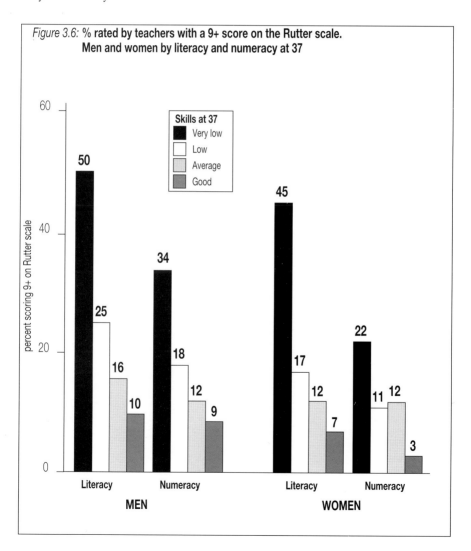

Figure 3.6: % rated by teachers with a 9+ score on the Rutter scale. Men and women by literacy and numeracy at 37

School characteristics

The great majority of students (93%) attended a local authority funded secondary school: 55% went to a comprehensive school, 23% to a secondary modern/technical school, 14% to a grammar school, 6% to an independent school, 1% to a special needs school and 1% to 'other' schools. Type of school attended differed by adult basic skills group. Figure 3.7 shows that no adults with very low literacy had been to a grammar or independent school (4% of adults with very low numeracy), 90% had either a comprehensive or secondary modern education. Nine percent went to a special needs school, as did 3% of adults with very low numeracy. In sharp contrast, approximately one-third of adults with good literacy or numeracy attended grammar or independent schools.

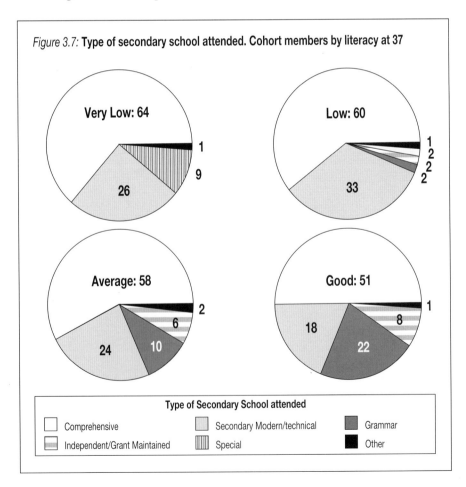

Figure 3.7: **Type of secondary school attended. Cohort members by literacy at 37**

Four in five grammar or independent schools were single sex, in comparison with 1 in 10 comprehensive schools. Given that the different types of secondary school were selecting their intake on the basis of cognitive test scores, it followed that attendance at single sex secondary schools similarly differed between adult basic skills groups. Just 1 in 10 men and women with very low literacy skills attended a single sex school, in comparison with one-third of men and women with good literacy. Those most likely to have attended a single sex secondary school were women with good numeracy: 45%.

The selectiveness of the schools the cohort members attended, was evident further in the social class composition of the school. Far fewer cohort members with poor skills went to a school with a preponderance of middle class children. Forty percent of cohort members with good adult literacy or numeracy at 37 had gone to a secondary school where more than 50% of the fathers were in non-manual occupations. This compared with 10% of those with very low adult literacy or numeracy at 37.

At the time the cohort members were attending secondary schools, 'streaming' by academic performance was the common basis for school organisation – 75% of the cohort were streamed for English, and 89% for maths classes between age 12-13. Slightly more men and women with very low literacy or numeracy at 37 had been allocated to classes via streaming, i.e. they were likely to have been grouped with students who had similar skills. As the two tier examination structure of GCE and CSE was in place at this time, allocation to a particular 'stream' most often decided which exam, if any, was to be taken at age 16. Potential was decided early on. At age 11, teachers were asked to assess the 'GCE potential' of all eleven year olds in the cohort members' school. Almost half of those with very low literacy (46%) and two fifths (40%) of those with very low numeracy went to a school where less than 20% of their peers were thought to be GCE candidates. Far fewer adults, around 1 in 4, with good literacy (28%) or numeracy (26%) attended such schools.

Of those cohort members who had been 'streamed', 4% of those streamed by their competence at English were assigned to a 'non-exam' course, as were 7% of adults streamed by their maths skills. For adults with very low literacy, 20% followed a 'non-exam' English course and 33% a 'non-exam' maths course. Despite this teacher judgement of lack of potential, only 17% of those with very low adult literacy had attended remedial English classes and 6% with very low adult numeracy had received remedial maths tuition.

Parental interest in their child's education

Far fewer parents of those cohort members with very low basic skills in adulthood had wanted them to remain at school after the minimum leaving age of 16 – typically a repetition of their own early age of leaving – and very few teachers held the view that these parents had much interest in the educational progress of their child. At age 7 teachers felt unable to assess the interest of 7% of mothers and 37% of fathers, with a slightly higher proportion for the parents of cohort members with poor adult basic skills. It is probably safe to assume that for the majority this resulted from a lack of parent-teacher contact during the year. Fathers traditionally become more involved with their child's education when they reach secondary school. Thus at age 16 a much lower 17% of fathers now fell into the 'unable to say' category, but differences between adult basic skills groups were now apparent. Teachers were now unable to comment on the interest of 24% of fathers of those with very low literacy, 14% with good literacy.

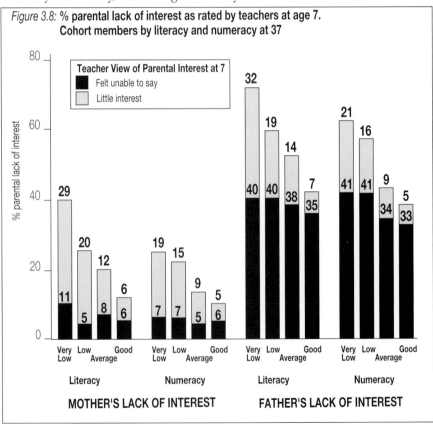

Figure 3.8: % parental lack of interest as rated by teachers at age 7. Cohort members by literacy and numeracy at 37

More significantly, differences in the percentage of parents reported as having 'little interest' in their child's education *increased* as the child got older between the very low and good literacy and numeracy groups. Figure 3.8 shows that 29% of mothers and 32% of fathers of those with very low literacy had shown 'little interest' in their education when they were 7, as did 19% of mothers and 21% of fathers of those with very low numeracy. This compared with between 5% to 7% of mothers and fathers of adults with good literacy or numeracy. By age 16, 39% of mothers and 48% of fathers of adults with very low literacy were rated by teachers as showing 'little interest' in their education. In contrast, just 6% of mothers and 7% of fathers of those with good literacy were rated with little interest.

Summary and conclusions

The whole education experience of adults with basic skills difficulties differed from that of adults with good literacy and numeracy. They were the least likely in the cohort to have been read to as a child. Based on teachers' reports, they were less likely to have experienced teaching of phonics and basic numberwork by age $5^1/_2$. They attended schools where academic achievement and future aspirations were relatively low. Cognitive ability tests taken at 7 showed that adults with literacy and numeracy difficulties had struggled at the first stage of their formal education. They tended to perform poorly in the tests at 7 and by the time they were 11, when they were tested again, the gap between their performance and peers without skills difficulties was wider. Although more of those with poor basic skills were assessed as needing special help when they were at school, substantial proportions had not received any. Parents of those with poor skills were rated by teachers as less interested in their children's educational progress than those with good skills. At age 16 more of the adults with skills difficulties were assessed with a behavioural disorder on the Rutter scale (Rutter et al, 1970), and truanting was common. Although the vast majority of all cohort members (93%) attended a local authority funded secondary school, the composition of the comprehensive and secondary modern schools they did attend was heavily biased towards manual family intakes and against high numbers taking public examinations at 16. Similarly, cohort members with poor adult literacy and numeracy tended to have been located in the non-examination school streams.

- As early as age 7, men and women with very low skills at 37 had the lowest average reading and maths scores. By age 11, men with very low literacy in adulthood scored half that of men with good literacy in the reading test; in the maths test, the average 11 year score of men with very low numeracy was one third that of men with good numeracy.

- 40% of adults with very low literacy or very low numeracy were thought not to have had (respectively) reading or maths difficulties by their teachers at age 7, compared with 89% of adults with good literacy and 88% with good numeracy.

- In the opinion of teachers 26% of those with very low literacy skills as adults needed additional help at age 7 but did not receive it. 12% received help and 2% attended a special school.

- More parents of adults with very low literacy (29% mothers, 32% fathers) or very low numeracy (19% mothers, 21% fathers) were rated by teachers as showing 'little interest' in their education when they were 7. By age 16, 39% of mothers and 48% of fathers of adults with very low literacy were rated by teachers as showing 'little interest' in their education. In contrast, just 6% of mothers and 7% of fathers of cohort members with good literacy had parents who were rated as showing little interest.

- 64% of men and 71% of women with very low literacy truanted from school at age 16. This compared with 47% of men and 43% of women with good literacy.

- No adults with very low literacy and just 4% with very low numeracy had been to a grammar or independent school, compared with 33% of adults with good literacy or good numeracy.

CHAPTER 4

Transition from School to Work

Introduction

Failure to acquire the basic skills at school leads to negative educational outcomes later on. Such children typically fail to achieve more than minimal qualifications from the education system at age 16 and leave it at the minimum age. How far they succeed in getting the jobs they seek will depend on how accommodating the labour market is to people with poor education. At the time the cohort members left school in 1974, there was still a lot of unskilled and semi-skilled work available. So most were able to get a job. However, the range of opportunities was limited and becoming more restricted throughout the whole period of the 1970s. As the labour market massively re-structured at the beginning of the 1980s, unskilled jobs became even more scarce and many people lost their jobs. The question arises: to what extent did these early labour market experiences affect basic skills in adulthood? What characterised those with very poor basic skills in terms of labour market aspirations and early employment and training experiences?

Qualifications and early job expectations

Given their experiences within the education system, it was not surprising that most of the cohort members with poor basic skills left full-time education at the earliest opportunity with minimal qualifications. Two thirds of the NCDS cohort left full-time education at 16, but among those with very low adult literacy or numeracy, the fraction rose to nine tenths of the men and three quarters of the women.

Only 16% of the cohort ended compulsory education without at least one formal qualification, however poor the quality. But among the majority who left the education system at 16, this increased to 25% of men and 20% of women. In figure 4.1 we see that even at age 23, 64% of men and 67% of women with very low literacy, 49% of men and 44% of women with very low numeracy were still without any formal qualifications. This compared with only 15% of men and 13% of women with good literacy, and 10% of men and women with good numeracy.

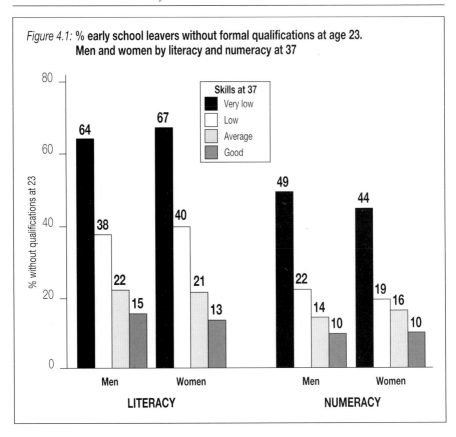

Figure 4.1: % early school leavers without formal qualifications at age 23. Men and women by literacy and numeracy at 37

Those adults with poor basic skills leaving school with no qualifications had little to offer future employers. Access to many areas of work was severely restricted. What were the occupational aspirations of these cohort members when they were children? When just eleven years old, they were asked to imagine that they were twenty-five and to say what they thought they would be doing in their work and home life when they grew up. Answers varied a lot, with some children writing a lengthy passage, others a few words, but just 1% of boys and 2% of girls did not mention their 'job'. Even these imagined jobs differed by skills groups. Figure 4.2a and 4.2b give the more obvious differences in proposed future employment by gender. Far more of those with good adult basic skills anticipated a professional career. Men with poor adult basic skills were more likely to cite a skilled or semi-skilled manual occupation, or that they would become professional sportsmen. Women with poor adult basic skills were more likely to see themselves finding work within the 'personal services', or taking on full-time home-care responsibilities.

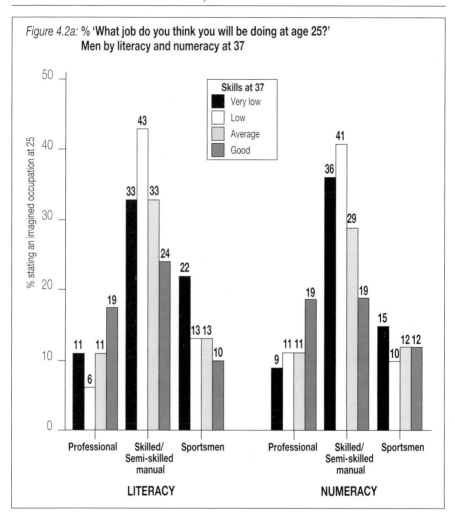

Figure 4.2a: % 'What job do you think you will be doing at age 25?'
Men by literacy and numeracy at 37

First employment experiences of early school leavers

What were the first labour market experiences of the early school leavers? Men and women with poor skills were far less likely to have served an apprenticeship or to have received 'quality' work-related training (amounting to either 100+ hours or for two weeks) in their early careers. What sort of jobs did they enter, and what opportunities for training were provided?

In table 4.1 we see that early school leavers with good literacy and numeracy spent an average of 3.9 years (men) and between 3.2 to 3.3 years (women) in their first

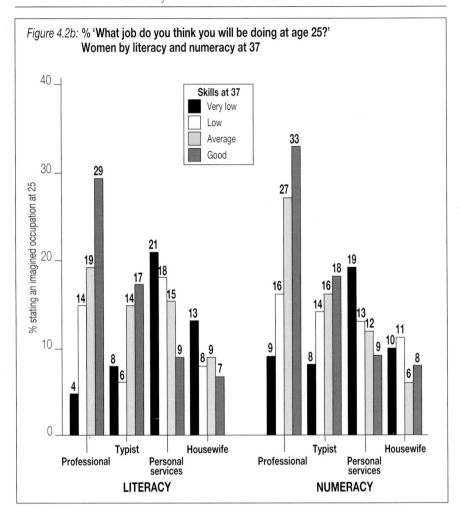

Figure 4.2b: % **'What job do you think you will be doing at age 25?'**
Women by literacy and numeracy at 37

job: men and women with poor skills tended to have spent less time in it. Men with very low literacy had spent only 3.1 years on average in their first job and women with very low literacy as little as 1.9 years.

Low grade work was the norm for many. Figure 4.3a shows that 39% of men with very low literacy and 31% of men with very low numeracy went into unskilled or semi-skilled manual work after leaving education at 16. This compared with no more than 16% of men with good literacy or numeracy who entered the workforce at 16.

Table 4.1: *Average number of years spent in a first job by early school leavers – Men and women by literacy and numeracy at 37*

	Men				Women			
	Literacy	*sd*	Numeracy	*sd*	Literacy	*sd*	Numeracy	*sd*
Very Low	3.1	2.8	3.4	2.8	1.9	2.2	2.9	2.5
Low	3.1	2.6	3.5	2.7	3.0	2.9	3.1	2.7
Average	3.7	2.7	3.8	2.7	3.2	2.5	3.1	2.4
Good	3.9	2.8	3.9	2.8	3.2	2.6	3.3	2.7

Although women were less likely to take up low grade manual work (less than 1% went into unskilled manual work at 16), Figure 4.3b shows comparable differences in first occupation between basic skills groups. 53% of women with very low

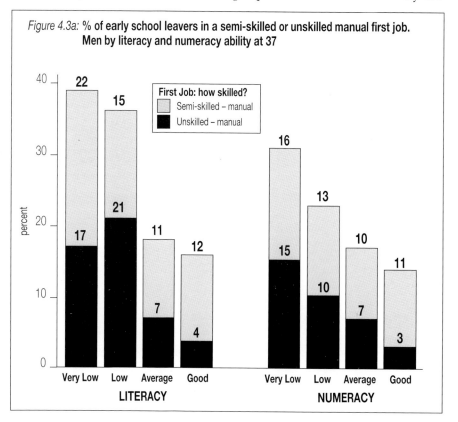

Figure 4.3a: % of early school leavers in a semi-skilled or unskilled manual first job. Men by literacy and numeracy ability at 37

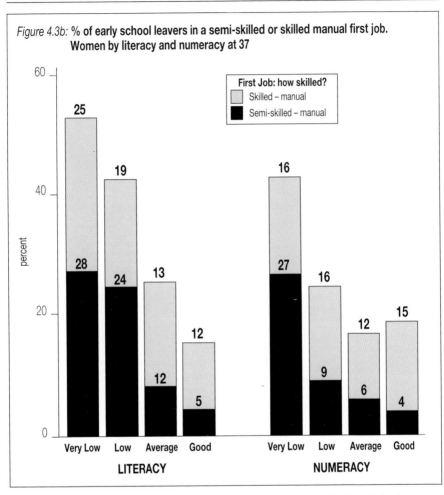

Figure 4.3b: % of early school leavers in a semi-skilled or skilled manual first job. Women by literacy and numeracy at 37

literacy and 43% with very low numeracy went into semi-skilled or skilled manual work. This compared with just 17% of women with good literacy and 19% with good numeracy who also left full-time education at 16.

The most highly regarded destination for early school leavers in the 1958 cohort was apprenticeship, especially for boys, because of the high quality training it was considered to provide. Only a minority of cohort members with very low basic skills had served an apprenticeship or received other kinds of quality training of two weeks or 100 hours duration: 52% of men and 75% of women with very low literacy had *never* received any training of this kind compared with only 11% of men and 45% of women with good literacy.

Of those cohort members who did not receive quality training in their early careers, but reported basic training in their first job, men and women with poor literacy and numeracy were again worst off. They were far more likely to have only received induction training when first starting work – i.e., they were *'shown the ropes'*. Only 35% of men with very low literacy and 40% of men with very low numeracy (who had received only basic training), went on to receive further training after their induction process. This compared with at least half of all other men who entered the workforce at 16. Women as a group received less basic training than men. For women with poor skills training was almost unknown. Only 11% of women with very low literacy and 19% with very low numeracy (who reported only basic training) had received anything more than induction type training at the start of their first job. This compared with 41% of women with good literacy and 44% of women with good numeracy. The foundations for a marginalised future had been firmly laid.

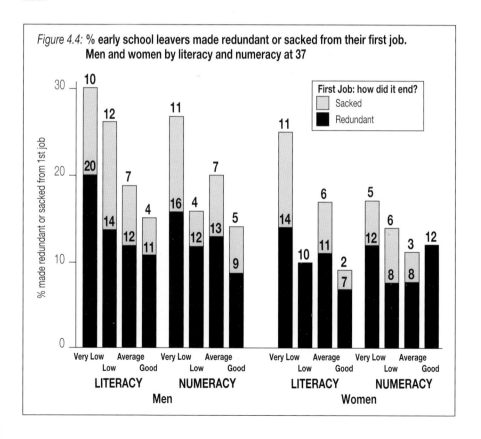

Figure 4.4: % **early school leavers made redundant or sacked from their first job. Men and women by literacy and numeracy at 37**

At age 23, around 25% of men and women had the same full-time job they had at 16. Only women with very low literacy were less likely to have been in one continuous job: just 13%. Leaving employment or changing an employer can be a positive or negative experience, depending very much on the circumstances bringing about the change. So, what was the reason that early school leavers left their first full-time job? Figure 4.4 shows that men and women with very low literacy or numeracy were more likely to cite redundancy or being sacked in comparison with the others. Differences between the adult basic skills groups were more distinct for men: twice as many men with very low literacy or numeracy had been made redundant or sacked from their first job in comparison with men who had good skills: 30% to 15% for literacy, 27% to 14% for numeracy.

Youth unemployment

Taking redundancies and sackings together, a higher percentage of men and women with poor skills had to look for another job before they were ready to. How did they fare? Youth unemployment was not as widely experienced in the late 1970s as it became in the early to mid 1980s, but what there was tended to be concentrated among those with poor qualifications and skills.

Figure 4.5 shows that between 16 and 23 men with very low literacy or numeracy skills were *four* times as likely to have experienced two or more years of *accumulated* unemployment as the men with good literacy or any other level of numeracy (12% to 3% literacy, 11% to 3% numeracy). Moreover, men with very low literacy or numeracy were far more likely to have suffered long-term unemployment – defined as a continuous spell of at least one year. This was highest for men with very low literacy (20%), and lowest for men with good numeracy (4%).

Given the different relationships men and women have with the labour market, fewer women had been categorised as unemployed for two years or more in their early careers. However, women with poor basic skills were more likely to have experienced unemployment for an *accumulated* time of at least one year between age 16 to 23. As with men, this was highest for women with very low literacy (18%), lowest for women with good numeracy (2%).

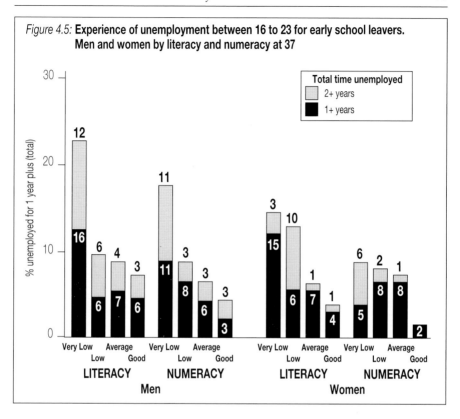

Figure 4.5: **Experience of unemployment between 16 to 23 for early school leavers. Men and women by literacy and numeracy at 37**

Summary and conclusions

Disadvantaged by their poor educational achievements, many more of the men and women with poor basic skills left school at the earliest opportunity, and the great majority still had no formal qualifications at 23. When they were 11 most boys with poor basic skills had aspirations to work in manual occupations, though 'sportsman' was also popular. The most popular occupational choices for girls with poor skills were in the 'personal services', or being 'at home' full-time. In reality, unskilled or semi-skilled low grade work was the common destination for most of these early school leavers lacking basic skills. Few received even basic *'on the job'* training and many more experienced long term unemployment, redundancy and being sacked.

- Among early school leavers, 52% of men and 75% of women with very low literacy had not entered into apprenticeships – the quality training of the mid-1970s – compared with 11% of men and 45% of women with good literacy.

- Twice as many men with very low literacy or very low numeracy had been made redundant or sacked from their first job compared with their counterparts who had good skills (30% to 15% literacy; 27% to 14% numeracy).

- Between 16 and 23, men with very low literacy or very low numeracy were four times as likely to have experienced two or more years of unemployment as men who had good literacy or any other level of numeracy (12% to 3% literacy, 11% to 3% numeracy). Women with very low literacy were more than three times as likely to have been unemployed for one year or more as women who had good literacy (18% to 5%).

CHAPTER 5

Adult Working Life

Introduction

The previous section took us across the period of life between 16 and 23 when most cohort members were beginning to find their feet in employment. The next phase of the study ran between 23 and 33. We use the data collected at 33 to discover what if anything else in employment appeared to relate to the basic skills problems at 37.

Highest qualification at 33

Men and women continued their pursuit of education and qualifications in their thirties – even the early school leavers and those with poor basic skills. By age 33, the percentage of men and women without any formal qualifications had dropped in all literacy and numeracy groups. Perhaps surprisingly, women with very low skills were among the most likely to have gained some sort of qualification (at least at NVQ1 level) between age 23 and 33. Among early school leavers, only 5% of men and 4% of women with *good* numeracy and 9% of men and 8% of women with *good* literacy were *without* formal qualifications at 33. Although the percentage was far higher for men and women with poor basic skills, a relatively low 35% of women and 41% of men with very low numeracy, who had left full-time education at 16, were without formal qualifications. Men and women with very low literacy remained by far the most likely not to have any formal qualifications: 60% and 58% respectively .

Labour market participation

Turning to participation in the labour market, differences between the adult basic skills groups were very apparent. Although over 50% of all women had spent at least a year in a full-time home-care role between age 23 to 33, only 6% had spent all ten years at home. This increased for women with poor basic skills: 12% with very low numeracy, 9% with very low literacy and 15% with low literacy had been in a full-time home-care role for all of this time. In Figure 5.2 we see that women

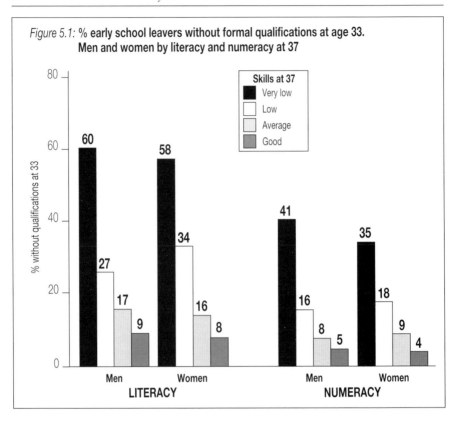

Figure 5.1: % early school leavers without formal qualifications at age 33. Men and women by literacy and numeracy at 37

with very low literacy (55%) or numeracy skills (38%) were at least three times as likely to have never held a full-time job between 23 and 33, as women with good skills (15% literacy, 12% numeracy). Just 14% of women with very low numeracy had been in continuous full-time employment during this time, compared with 33% of women with good numeracy.

Figure 5.2 also shows that men with very low literacy or numeracy were up to 5 times as likely not to have held a full-time job at any time between 23 and 33 in comparison with men who had good literacy or numeracy (18% to 4% literacy, 16% to 3% numeracy). Three-quarters of men with good skills (75% literacy, 76% numeracy) had always been in full-time work during this time. This contrasted with just under 60% of men with very low skills (58% literacy, 57% numeracy). Long term unemployment was also more common for men with poor basic skills: 7% with very low numeracy had been unemployed for five or more years, compared with less than 1% of men with good numeracy.

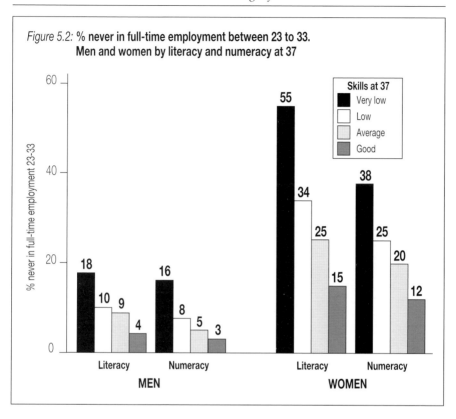

Figure 5.2: % never in full-time employment between 23 to 33. Men and women by literacy and numeracy at 37

Work-related training

Men and women with poor basic skills were far less likely to have had work-related training from an employer. For those who had ever been employed between 23 to 33, 66% of men with very low literacy and 59% of men with very low numeracy had not received any work related training from an employer. This was in sharp contrast to the 36% of men with good literacy and 31% with good numeracy who had not received training.

Women with poor skills who had ever worked fared even worse than men. Three quarters of women with either very low literacy (78%) or very low numeracy (75%) had never received training from an employer. Women with good numeracy were most likely to have had training: 65% *had* received it, with a third of these women having been on at least two 3-day training courses.

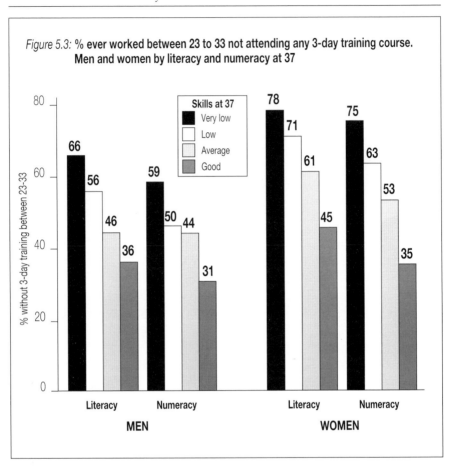

Figure 5.3: % ever worked between 23 to 33 not attending any 3-day training course. Men and women by literacy and numeracy at 37

Summary and conclusions

By age 33, although some men and women with poor skills had managed to gain qualifications, those with very low literacy skills were still far the most likely to have no qualifications. Differences in labour market experiences remained very apparent between skills groups. More women with poor skills took on long term home-care responsibilities, while poorly skilled men experienced long term unemployment. For those who had ever been employed between age 23 and 33, men and women with poor literacy and numeracy were again unlikely to have received any work-related training. For those that did, the quality was of a much lower standard. Women who had ever worked fared less well than men, but those with poor skills fared the worst.

- Women with very low literacy or numeracy skills were at least three times as likely to have never held a full-time job between 23 and 33, as women with good skills (55% to 15% literacy, 38% to 12% numeracy). Just 14% of women with very low numeracy had been in continuous full-time employment during this time, as were 33% of women with good numeracy.

- 5 times as many men with very low literacy or numeracy skills had not held a full-time job between 23 and 33 as men who had good skills (18% to 4% literacy, 16% to 3% numeracy). During the same time, 7% of men with very low numeracy had been unemployed for five or more years, compared with less than 1% of men with good numeracy.

- 66% of men with very low literacy skills and 59% of men with very low numeracy skills had not received any work-related training from an employer. By contrast, 36% of men with good literacy and 31% with good numeracy had not received training; those with training had usually attended at least two 3-day training courses.

CHAPTER 6

Origins of Adult Basic Skills Difficulties?

Introduction

The previous chapters have demonstrated strong relationships between circumstances and experiences earlier in life with basic skills performance in adulthood. The question arises as to whether many of these influences are all measuring much the same factor in the development of the basic skills, or whether they represent relatively independent influences on basic skills acquisition. The further question that arises is what, in combination, all of them can tell us about the origins of basic skills difficulties. How much of the variation between the cohort members' scores on our basic skills tests at age 37 can be accounted for in terms of these early factors? What is it *in total* that characterises those who have *good* literacy and numeracy scores as opposed to those whose scores are *very low*?

To answer these questions we use the multivariate statistical technique, multiple regression. The technical details need not concern us here, but basically multiple regression enables us to do two things. First it tells us how much of the variation in an outcome measure, such as a basic skills score, can be predicted or accounted for, in terms of the influences to which people have been subjected, such as circumstances at home and experiences at school. The answer is given in terms of a single 'multiple correlation coefficient' (R), which is similar to the simple correlation coefficient giving the strength of relationship between two variables that we encountered earlier. R gives the correlation between the literacy or numeracy outcome score and the whole set of earlier circumstances or experiences. R^2 tells us the proportion of variation in adult basic skills scores that has been explained.

The second outcome from multiple regression analysis, is a measure of how strongly each of the early influences relate to the later outcome – the adult literacy or numeracy score, *holding constant* the effects of all other influences. In other words, all other things being equal, how well does parents reading to children predict adult literacy performance: how *important*, relative to other variables, is parents reading to children in *explaining* adult literacy? The measure of strength of relationship used is called a regression coefficient, which, in the standardised form used here, is just like a correlation coefficient, and has a range of between –1 and +1.

In the sections that follow, the results of the multiple regression analysis, carried out separately for men and women, are presented in a number of stages. First of all we build up the explanation of adult basic skills performances by examining the connection between the literacy and numeracy test scores and family characteristics at birth. We then see to what extent we can improve our explanation of these performances by bringing in variables representing influences up to age 7. We then move on to add in variables measured up to age 11, up to age 16, then up to age 23 and finally up to age 33.

Our first interest is in determining whether there is a point when there is no further improvement in the explanation gained by adding other variables – no more of the variation in the adult literacy and numeracy scores can be explained. Is there an age or stage of life when the explanation can no longer be improved by bringing in further possible influences?

Secondly we want to find out which variables, (representing the influences), feature most strongly in the explanation. In each case we will expect the variables that have been measured more recently, i.e. later in the cohort members' lives, to be the stronger predictors, often replacing those influences we identified earlier. In this sense, variables that do retain their predictive powers from very early on in life right into adulthood are a major focus of interest: they point to key stumbling blocks which educational intervention needs to address at an early age. Other variables will tend to be overtaken by the variables measured later, particularly those to do with educational performance.

Thus we might find that up to the age of 7 parents reading to children predicts adult literacy, but after that reading performance at primary school itself becomes the major predictor and the parents' reading as an influence disappears. To deal with this absorption of early influence into school performance outcomes, a second set of analyses is presented which examines these earlier school performances themselves through multiple regression methods. Thus instead of using adult literacy and numeracy test scores as the outcome variables, we examine as outcomes reading and maths scores as measured at 7, 11 and 16. This approach enables us to ascertain in more precise detail how the various circumstances and influences in childhood produce the outcome which is most likely to lead to the adult basic skills problem.

Finally, in interpreting the significance of individual explanatory variables we need to be aware that many of them are correlated among themselves. In multiple regression, different explanatory variables 'compete' with each other as predictors and one of them from a correlated set is likely to emerge as the main predictor. This means that we need to treat the identified main predictors as indicators of broad sets of influences to do with circumstances and experiences at home or at school rather than as important in their own right.

The full sets of regression coefficients and the proportions of variation explained in each analysis are shown in Appendix 4 (adult literacy and numeracy outcomes) and Appendix 5 (earlier cognitive ability outcomes).

Accounting for adult literacy and numeracy scores

The explanatory variables used in the multiple regression analyses have been discussed in the previous chapters. Table 6. 1 displays them in the order in which they entered the multiple regression analysis, i.e. starting at birth and moving up through the various stages of childhood, youth and young adulthood.

How much of the variation in adult literacy and numeracy scores can be explained?

Figures 6.1a and 6.1b plot the percentages of variation explained in numeracy and literacy scores by the analysis against age at which the measurements of the explanatory variables were taken: birth, 7, 11, 16, 23 and 33 for men and women respectively.

Even at birth a small percentage of the variation in numeracy and literacy scores (highest at 6% for numeracy) could be explained by circumstances prevailing at this time. From then on the percentages of variation explained increased rapidly, rising to 34% in the case of women's numeracy scores through the primary school period to age 11. The rise continued, but at a lower rate, through the early stages of secondary school and then levelled off, but not entirely, at the school leaving age 16. From 16 to 33 a further 4% to 5% of the variance was explained in numeracy and literacy scores for men; during the same period an additional 2% of the variation was explained in both numeracy and literacy scores for women. By age 33 the maximum figure of 42% of variation in women's numeracy scores could be explained.

Table 6.1: *Explanatory variables involved in the series of multiple regression analyses with adult literacy and numeracy scores as dependent variables*

At birth	Up to 7	Up to 11	Up to 16	Up to 23	Up to 33
At birth Age mother left full-time education Social class Birthweight	At birth Age mother left full-time education Social class Birthweight **At age 7** Reading test Maths test Draw-a-man test Parental interest in child education: teacher rated Mother read to child School attendance Overcrowding in the home (-) Rented housing	At birth Age mother left full-time education Social class Birthweight **At age 7** Reading test Maths test Draw-a-man test Copying Design test Parental interest in child education: teacher rated Mother read to child School attendance Overcrowding in the home (-) Rented housing **At age 11** Reading test Maths test Parental interest in child education: teacher rated % students in school GCE standard School attendance Overcrowding in the home (-) Rented housing Free school meals (-)	At birth Age mother left full-time education Social class Birthweight **At age 7** Reading test Maths test Draw-a-man test Copying Design test Parental interest in child education: teacher rated Mother read to child School attendance Overcrowding in the home (-) Rented housing **At age 11** Reading test Maths test Parental interest in child education: teacher rated % students in school GCE standard School attendance Overcrowding in the home (-) Rented housing Free school meals (-) **At age 16** Reading test Maths test Public Exam results Parent-Teacher meetings Parental interest in child education: teacher rating Single sex school Truancy Rutter score: teacher rated (-) School attendance % dad's in school non-manual jobs Rented housing Overcrowded accommodation (-) How many share the bedroom (-)	At birth Age mother left full-time education Social class Birthweight **At age 7** Reading test Maths test Draw-a-man test Copying Design test Parental interest in child education: teacher rated Mother read to child School attendance Overcrowding in the home (-) Rented housing **At age 11** Reading test Maths test Parental interest in child education: teacher rated % students in school GCE standard School attendance Overcrowding in the home (-) Rented housing Free school meals (-) **At age 16** Reading test Maths test Public Exam results Parent-Teacher meetings Parental interest in child education: teacher rating Single sex school Truancy (-) Rutter score: teacher rated (-) School attendance % dad's in school non-manual jobs Rented housing Overcrowded accommodation (-) How many share the bedroom (-) **At Age 23** Age left full-time education Highest qualification at at 23 Work-related training: up to 23 *Between 16 - 23:* Months employed Months unemployed (-) Months in f/t home-care(-)	At birth Age mother left full-time education Social class Birthweight **At age 7** Reading test Maths test Draw-a-man test Copying Design test Parental interest in child education: teacher rated Mother read to child School attendance Overcrowding in the home (-) Rented housing **At age 11** Reading test Maths test Parental interest in child education: teacher rated % students in school GCE standard School attendance Overcrowding in the home (-) Rented housing Free school meals (-) **At age 16** Reading test Maths test Public Exam results Parent-Teacher meetings Parental interest in child education: teacher rating Single sex school Truancy (-) Rutter score: teacher rated (-) School attendance % dad's in school non-manual jobs Rented housing Overcrowded accommodation (-) How many share the bedroom(-) **At Age 23** Age left full-time education Highest qualification at 23 Work-related training: up to 23 *Between 16 - 23:* Months employed Months unemployed (-) Months in f/t home-care (-) **At Age 33** Highest qualification at 33 Work-related training: 23-33 *Between 23 - 33:* Months in f/t employment Months unemployed (-) Months in f/t home-care (-)

(-) = negative effect eg. the more overcrowded a home, the lower the adult literacy or numeracy score.

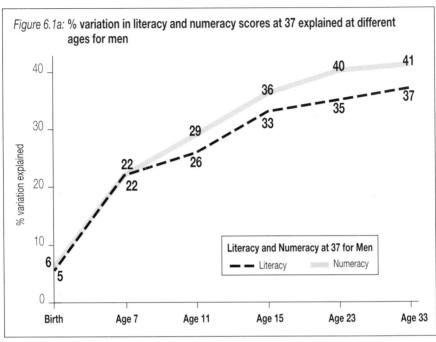

Figure 6.1a: % variation in literacy and numeracy scores at 37 explained at different ages for men

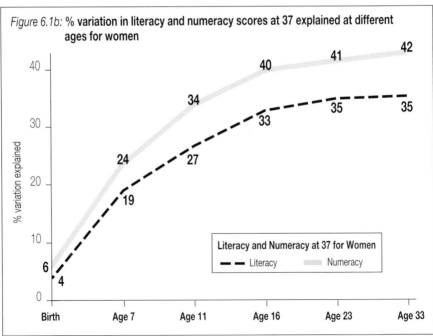

Figure 6.1b: % variation in literacy and numeracy scores at 37 explained at different ages for women

At every age point the percentage of explained variation was higher for numeracy than for literacy and higher overall for women then for men. This suggests that at least in terms of the kinds of explanatory variables measured in NCDS, numeracy was the more sensitive outcome measure, i.e. it was more easily explained. Similarly the explanatory variables accounted better for women's numeracy scores, but not their literacy scores, than they did men's: women's scores were the more predictable in terms of earlier circumstances and experiences. How do we account for the variation in adult literacy and numeracy scores that remains unexplained by the earlier circumstances and experiences included in the analysis? A proportion of this unexplained variation is likely to be due to measurement error: we cannot assess people's experiences and performance as accurately as we would like. The remainder is likely to be due to individual life patterns which cannot be explained in statistical terms. Although much of the difference in adult basic skills is predictable, some of it is not.

In summary the analysis points, as perhaps we might expect, to primary school as the critical period for acquisition of the basic skills. But their continuing susceptibility to influence is still apparent through the early stages of secondary school into early adulthood. This constitutes powerful evidence for the value of continuing basic skills education in adult life.

Most important influences on literacy and numeracy skills at 37

At birth

The higher the social class at birth the better the performance in the literacy and numeracy assessments at 37. This relationship was particularly strong with numeracy scores – for both men and women. Mother's age at leaving full-time education also predicted literacy and numeracy scores for men, but only numeracy scores for women.

Up to 7

As we have seen, the predictive power of the regression model substantially increased with the inclusion of explanatory variables measured up to age 7. Social class at birth remained a significant predictor of adult basic skills, but the strength of this relationship had diminished. Strongest predictors of a good performance in the literacy and numeracy assessments were now the four cognitive tests: reading, maths and visual motor skills (*draw-a-man* and *copying designs* tests). Gender differences in the importance of the different types of early cognitive performance were apparent. As we might expect, reading test scores were the strongest predictor of adult literacy for both men and women. But although maths performance at 7 was the strongest predictor of men's adult numeracy, for women, *reading* performance at 7 was the better predictor of their adult *numeracy*. Conversely, maths performance at 7 had no bearing on women's literacy, but was a strong predictor for men. Copying design test scores were a strong predictor of literacy and numeracy for both men and women; draw-a-man test results predicted adult numeracy for both men and women, but literacy just for women.

Other than the early cognitive measures, parental interest in their child's education (teacher rated) predicted good adult literacy and numeracy performances for both men and women. For women, being read to by their mother at a younger age also predicted their adult literacy and numeracy, as did school attendance predict good literacy. For men, overcrowding in the home predicted *poor* literacy and numeracy performances at 37.

Up to 11

Larger gender differences emerged once information present at age 11 was incorporated into the analyses. Although the strength of the overall relationship between circumstances and experiences up to age 11 and adult literacy and numeracy remained similar for men and women, a more diverse set of experiences now helped explain literacy and numeracy differences among women. Other than direct measures of cognitive ability, only a few other variables predicted adult literacy or numeracy for men.

Reading performance and copying design skills at 7, both cognitive tests and free school meals at 11 (a good indirect measure of the financial circumstances of a family) all strongly predicted adult literacy scores for both men and women. Maths performance at 7 was important for men. For women, parental support, as indicated by the interest in education of their parents and being read to by their mother at an early age, together with school attendance, continued to predict a good literacy performance.

For adult numeracy, maths performance at 11 (and to a lesser extent at 7) was the only predictor common to men and women. For women, the measures of parental support (being read to by their mother at an early age and parental interest at 7) continued to have an impact on their numeracy score. Early reading ability similarly remained important, while family disadvantage (as indicated by receipt of free school meals at 11) predicted a *poor* performance. For men, predictors of good adult numeracy were copying design skills, maths performance and good school attendance at 7. Overcrowding in the home at 7 continued to predict *poor* numeracy in adulthood.

Up to 16

The strength of the overall relationship between early experiences and adult basic skills continued to rise through secondary school, but at a slower rate than in primary school. Again there was a big gender difference in the significant predictors of adult literacy and numeracy: reading and maths performance at 16 were the only new predictors of both adult scores common to both sexes. Copying design skills at 7 (literacy) and maths ability at 11 (numeracy) were the other cognitive measures to predict adult scores for both sexes. For women, reading ability at 7, maths ability at 11 and public examination results at 16 independently predicted adult literacy and numeracy. For men, maths score and copying design skills at 7 predicted performance in both adult tests.

The other predictors of a good literacy performance for women were different measures of parental support – parental interest at 7, being read to at a young age, the number of parent-teacher meetings at 16 – and good school attendance. Disruptive behaviour (as measured on the Rutter scale) was a strong predictor of a *poor* performance. For men, parental interest at 16 and the percentage of fathers in a non-manual occupation at their secondary school predicted good adult literacy skills; overcrowding in the home was still indicative of a *poor* performance in the literacy assessment.

Once again, few *other* early experiences predicted adult numeracy. School attendance at 7 predicted a good performance, overcrowded home conditions at 7 predicted a *poor* performance for men; being read to as a child predicted good scores for women. The early involvement of parents in the education of girls continued to be very important.

Up to 23

By this stage, the ability of the analysis to explain more variation in adult literacy and numeracy scores was much reduced, though some new predictors did appear. Not unexpectedly, highest qualification gained by 23 predicted adult basic skills for both men and women, but reading test performance at 16 remained a stronger predictor particularly for literacy. Maths performance at 11 was a strong predictor of adult numeracy. Of the new explanatory variables introduced, work-related training predicted good adult literacy and numeracy scores for men, but only numeracy scores for women. Months spent in full-time employment between age 16 and age 23 was also important for women's literacy performance. Months unemployed during the same period was a predictor of *poor* numeracy for men. The role of the explanatory variables measured earlier tended to repeat existing patterns. Early cognitive performance maintained its independent relationship with adult literacy. Reading and copying design test scores at 7 predicted good skills for men and women. Family disadvantage (free school meals) continued to predict *poor* basic skills. For women, parental support factors throughout childhood, school attendance (at 7) and single-sex secondary education predicted good literacy. Disruptive school behaviour (at 16) predicted *poor* skills. For men, predictors of good literacy were parental interest (at 16) and the percentage of fathers in a non-manual occupation at their secondary school.

For numeracy, maths performance and public examination results at 16 also predicted numeracy for women; family disadvantage (free school meals) predicted *poor* numeracy. For men the 'draw-a-man' test score at 7 predicted good skills; overcrowding in the home at 7 and disruptive behaviour at 16 both predicted *poor* adult numeracy.

Up to 33

The final stage of the analysis brought in experiences based entirely in adulthood, those occurring between the mid 20s and early 30s. Although the overall proportion of variation explained was only marginally higher, highest qualifications at 33 and labour market experiences between the ages of 23 and 33 were significant predictors of adult literacy and numeracy. Months spent in full-time employment from 23 predicted good literacy scores for both men and women, and men's numeracy. Earlier training and youth unemployment (age 16 to 23) similarly remained as key predictors of men's numeracy. With respect to earlier influences, a near identical set of significant predictors of adult literacy and numeracy to those at 23, was evident.

To summarise, cognitive test scores at earlier ages and parent interest and support were positively related to adult literacy and numeracy. Family disadvantage and evidence of behavioural difficulties at school appeared to work against their acquisition, with the effects being particularly prominent for women.

Explaining the key predictors

Running through the analysis just reported is the dominance of earlier cognitive performance, especially of reading and maths skills on later outcomes in adult literacy and numeracy, particularly for men. In one sense it might be thought not unreasonable for *only* these predictors to turn up continually as the key to basic skills failures, which makes it all the more interesting that so many other home

Table 6.2a *Early cognitive predictors of adult literacy*

| | Step 1 to 10 of analysis | | | | | | | | | |
	1	2	3	4	5	6	7	8	9	10
Sex	.10	.10	.11	.11	.15	.13	.12	.12	.11	.11
Age mother left full-time education		.11	.10	.09	.06	.03	.01	.00	-.02	-.02
Mother read to child			.10	.11	.09	.08	.06	.06	.06	.06
Draw-a-man test at 7				.20	.11	.07	.05	.05	.05	.05
Reading test at 7					.31	.17	.13	.12	.11	.11
Reading test at 11						.29	.12	.09	.07	.07
Reading test at 16							.32	.29	.27	.26
Exam score at 16								.12	.05	.04
Highest qualification at 23									.16	.13
Highest qualification at 33										.09
R^2	1%	2%	3%	7%	16%	22%	27%	28%	31%	31%

Table 6.2b: *Early cognitive predictors of adult numeracy*

| | Step 1 to 10 of analysis | | | | | | | | | |
	1	2	3	4	5	6	7	8	9	10
Sex	.14	.15	.15	.15	.14	.13	.11	.12	.11	.11
Age mother left full-time education		.15	.14	.13	.10	.06	.03	.02	.01	.00
Mother read to child			.09	.10	.10	.08	.07	.07	.06	.06
Draw-a-man test at 7				.22	.14	.07	.07	.06	.06	.06
Maths test at 7					.28	.10	.07	.07	.07	.06
Maths test at 11						.42	.28	.25	.23	.22
Maths test at 16							.25	.21	.18	.18
Exam score at 16								.12	.07	.05
Highest qualification at 23									.16	.07
Highest qualification at 33										.13
R^2	2%	4%	5%	10%	17%	29%	33%	34%	36%	36%

circumstances and family support variables maintained their importance in the explanation right up to adulthood. We now give even more attention to these other explanatory variables by examining the relationship to the main cognitive outcome measures – reading and maths scores at age 7, 11 and 16. But first the role of the cognitive measures themselves needs to be more precisely established.

Tables 6.2a and 6.2b use regression coefficients to show how one cognitive predictor of adult literacy or numeracy respectively, tends to replace another at later stages of life. As a baseline, we start with the prediction of the adult literacy and numeracy scores from family characteristics at birth. Then we add in relevant cognitive test scores at 7, then at 11, then at 16, including public examination scores, then at 23 (highest qualification) and finally at 33 (highest qualification). Moving from left to right across the tables (step 1 to step 10 of the analysis), we see the effect of introducing each later variable in turn on the predictive power for the earlier variables already included. Thus in table 6.2b, we see that age mother left full-time education, a family background characteristic at birth, starts off with a reasonably strong regression coefficient of .15 (step 2) but by the time all the variables up to 33 have been brought into the analysis (step 10) its relationship to adult numeracy has been reduced to zero (.00). In other words, we can see a chain of influence running from parents' education through reading to the child to good adult literacy or numeracy, with each later influence in the chain largely, but not entirely, absorbing the effects of the earlier influences.

The two main points to note from table 6.2a and 6.2b are, first, the high proportions of variation in adult literacy and numeracy that can be attributed to these cognitive variables alone – over 30% – and secondly that the continual replacement of earlier variables by later ones does not continue up to age 33. Thus in the case of adult literacy at age 37, the reading test at 7 retains its importance above the level of the reading test at 11, being surpassed only by the even more dominant cognitive outcome variable – reading test at 16. Highest qualification at 23 and 33 fail to replace this 16 year reading score as the key predictor of adult literacy. For numeracy there is an even more striking result. This time the maths score at 11 turns out to be the more important, even than maths score at 16, in predicting the adult numeracy score at 37: again neither are replaced in importance by highest qualification at 23 or 33. Another interesting result from these tables is that highest qualification at 23 turned out to be the more important predictor for literacy whereas highest qualification at 33 held this role for numeracy. We may speculate that additional qualifications gained after 23, in such professions as accountancy, management, business administration, etc, tend to nourish numeracy more than literacy.

Cognitive Ability at 7

Turning now to the explanation of the critical cognitive performance variables, what is the relative importance of the other explanatory variables in explaining how these scores have been achieved? When we consider just the factors present at birth, only a little overall variation in cognitive ability at 7 was explained – the highest was 5% for boys' reading ability. Interestingly, mother's age at leaving full-time education was a significant predictor of maths *and* reading ability for men, but for neither maths nor reading among women.

When factors and influences present at 7 were included, the overall variation explained in reading scores increased to 15% for men and 16% for women, but was below 10% for the maths scores of both men and women. Parental interest in education, as rated by the child's teacher, was the strongest individual predictor of maths and reading scores for both men and women. School attendance predicted good early reading skills in men and women, and good maths skills in men. For men, mother's age at leaving full-time education remained a predictor of good maths *and* reading skills, with overcrowded accommodation predicting a *poor* reading performance. For women, the home environment appeared to have even more influence. Overcrowded accommodation was a strong predictor of *poor* reading skills; rented accommodation predicted *poor* reading and maths scores. More difficult to interpret, increased birthweight also predicted good maths skills in girls.

Cognitive Ability at 11

As we might expect, the inclusion of cognitive tests at 7 resulted in a substantial increase in the percentage of overall variation explained for maths and reading scores at age 11. It rose to over 40% – higher for maths than for reading, explaining 50% of the variation in maths scores for men.

Key individual predictors of cognitive skills differed somewhat by gender. Reading scores at 7 were the strongest predictor of reading scores at 11 for both men and women. On the other hand, although maths scores at 7 were the strongest predictor of maths skills at 11 for women, *reading skills* at 7 were the strongest predictor of men's performance in the maths test at 11. Motor co-ordination skills at 7 were significant predictors of maths and reading at 11 for men and women; a stronger relationship was evident with *draw-a-man* skills for women, and copying design skills for men. Parental interest at 11 (teacher rated) and the percentage of fellow students at school rated with GCE ability were also strong predictors of these 11 year reading and maths scores for both sexes, but they were particularly important for men at this stage in their cognitive development. Interestingly, parental interest at 7 retained an independent effect on reading and maths performance at 11 for men, but not women. Family social class at birth predicted maths skills of men and women, but only reading skills for women. Free school meals predicted *poor* reading skills for men.

Ability at 16

The earlier cognitive test scores continued to be the strongest predictors of later cognitive skills. Reading and maths scores at 11 were the main predictors of reading and maths scores at 16 respectively. Parental interest at 16 was significantly related to reading and maths performance at 16 in both men and women, with earlier parental interest (at 11) also retaining a positive relationship with maths skills for women.

Overall, *school factors* appeared to hold more importance in the prediction of the 16 year maths scores, while *material circumstances at home* appeared the more important predictors of reading scores at 16. The percentage of students' fathers in non-manual occupations at 16 replaced the teachers' estimate at age 11 of fellow students' GCE ability at 11 on cognitive skills, particularly for maths performance. Disruptive school behaviour as measured by the Rutter scale predicted poor cognitive skills at 16, with the relationship being particularly strong for the boys' maths scores. A low level of truancy also appeared important for developing good maths skills in men and women, as did attendance at a single sex secondary school for women. Family disadvantage, overcrowded and rented housing, were related to a *poor* reading performance for both men and women.

Key determinants of Adult Literacy and Numeracy problems

The multiple regression analysis helps us to identify the key influences on basic skills development at different stages of life and provides pointers to the kinds of processes that can enhance or impede their acquisition. These are summarised in table 6.3 together with targets for intervention. The earlier study of 21 year olds' basic skills problems in BCS70 pointed to family disadvantage early in life coupled with weak parental interest and support as critical in impeding basic skills development. The new study of 37 year olds born 12 years earlier reinforces this picture and adds new insights into the key influences of secondary school experience and the labour market.

Table 6.3: *Origins of adult basic skills difficulties and targets for intervention*

Life Stage	Critical Factors	Main Outcomes	Intervention Targets
pre-school	unskilled family parents' education poor no pre-school preparation	visual motor skills weak	pre-school preparation family disadvantage
early primary school	visual motor skills poor disadvantaged home background parents' interest low family support absent	reading skills weak	primary curriculum family disadvantage family literacy home school relations additional support
late primary school	reading poor disadvantaged home background parents' interest low	reading skills weak maths skills weak	
early secondary school	reading poor mathematics poor non-exam stream behaviour problems teacher expectations low parent interest low	reading skills weak maths skills weak examination potential low	secondary curriculum school/class organisation examinations policy home school relations student behaviour teacher expectations
late secondary school	basic skills poor no public exams non-exam stream school attendance poor behaviour problems teacher expectations low	reading skills weak maths skills weak public examinations not taken	
post 16	basic skills poor early leaving no qualifications no work based training unemployment	reading skills weak maths skills weak no academic qualifications no vocational qualifications	further ed. curriculum youth training first employment work-based training employers unemployment leisure life
adulthood	literacy and numeracy poor no further education or training no continuous employment unemployment	literacy poor numeracy poor no further vocational qualifications no professional qualifications	basic skills education further education and training work-based training unemployment parent education

The first steps to acquiring the basic skills lie in the visual motor skills gained through play activities at nursery school or at home. Reinforced by parental support through reading at home, and good home school relations, elementary reading follows and following reading, numberwork and maths. By the time they leave primary school most children have achieved proficiency in basic reading and maths. The next step in the process builds on the foundations that are now in place, with the basic skills of reading and maths advancing to the kinds of standards required in public examinations at 16. From then on there are small improvements through staying on in education to take 'A levels' and vocational qualifications. For those in work, training serves to reinforce and develop the basic skills further; as does time in full-time employment as opposed to unemployment or being 'at home'. Those who move on to further education at college or university, or attend professional training courses (especially those leading to qualifications) are also likely to strengthen their basic skills further.

This is the positive picture of the basic skills acquisition process. Its opposite is the downward cycle where children's and subsequently teenagers' and young adults' grasp of the basic skills remains poor or gets worse. The first set of influences impeding basic skills development is the material conditions of the home, often associated with low incomes reflected in free school meals for the children and rented, often overcrowded, housing. Parental interest in their child's education is judged by teachers to be lacking and the kinds of constructive play underpinning the visual motor skills – reading to the children and other forms of educational support that can be taken for granted in typical middle class homes – are similarly absent. The effects of these conditions persist through primary school and when the focus shifts more to the mathematical skills and their development these are even more impeded by the widening gap between home and school, especially among girls.

Secondary schooling is likely to begin badly, with experience of remedial education and classes with a high proportion of poor achievers in them the norm. Behavioural problems are common, heightening the alienation between student and teacher. There are limited expectations by teachers of the student's chances of success in public examinations at 16 and little encouragement to work hard for them, or even to sit them. Early leaving follows with the prospect of nothing much more than an unskilled job requiring only minimal training, a dead-end training scheme or unemployment. Lengthening spells of unemployment follow, interspersed with casual unskilled jobs, none of which makes good the earlier educational deficiencies. The consequence is continuing deficits in the basic skills persisting into adulthood, with few opportunities for the employment experiences that might help to mitigate them.

The policy challenge

This picture of 'virtuous' and 'vicious' circles is common in accounts of educational success and failure. It gains added significance for the acquisition of the basics skills: their absence will hold up the whole educational process, during school and after it. The challenge for policy is therefore how to reverse the vicious circle, if not at the earliest possible age, then through opportunities inside and outside the formal education and training systems. Although by the standards of research of this kind a remarkably large proportion of the variation in adult basic skill scores – approaching 50% – could be attributed to prior conditions and experiences, the fact that over 50% remained 'unexplained' suggests that at the individual level there is still much to play for. In other words the influences identified through our regression analyses indicated broad statistical tendencies for certain life factors and basic skills acquisition to go together. But these in themselves cannot encompass all the variety of individual life patterns through which school-based basic skills problems are mitigated. The fact that the length of time in employment and the experience of work based training explains some of the variation in adult literacy and numeracy points to a range of adult contexts in which the education process can continue to work. Other venues not covered in the survey such as youth clubs, particular forms of youth training, and modern apprenticeships, offer other opportunities for basic skills education.

Nevertheless the foundations of basics skills difficulties and the education failure that follows them are laid early in life which reinforces the importance of Basic Skills Agency initiatives of the *family literacy* kind. Engaging poor-reading parents directly in the task of teaching their children how to read is one attractive and successful way into this, which benefits parents as well as their children. But even earlier – and before the child's immersion into the large classes of primary school – the appropriate pre-school environments at home or at nursery school offer even better opportunities for developing the elementary foundations of cognitive skill on which learning to read is built.

The key role of visual motor skills in early reading underlines the value of constructive play of the kind that good pre-school education provides. Primary school class size may not feature among the factors accounting for adult literacy and numeracy problems, but that is almost certainly because by the time children enter primary school the damage has already been done. There is obviously no conscious intention on the part of parents, often struggling against difficult economic conditions, to restrict their children's access to the building blocks of basic skills learning, just lack of awareness of how to exercise their role as educators, a role which is taken for granted in most middle class homes. The importance of increased provision in the form of pre-school education at home or in kindergartens cannot be stated enough. This can ensure, perhaps more than anything else, that the foundations of the basic skills are in place for all children, not just those whose parents recognise their importance.

The final message that comes from this research therefore is to stress both the predictability and the fluidity of learning the basic skills. Keeping learning opportunities open at all ages, and at all stages, is not only the key to basic skills improvements but to establishment of the learning society itself.

Scoring the Literacy and Numeracy Assessments

Tasks in the literacy and numeracy assessments

Full details of the tasks used in the adult functional literacy and numeracy assessments are given in *It doesn't get any better* (Bynner and Parsons, 1997). Functional literacy was restricted to reading. Each task consisted of a visual stimulus, such as a page from 'yellow pages' or items to purchase from a shop, and a number of questions about it or exercises to be performed. Examples of the questions are given below.

Literacy

1. The cohort member is shown a newspaper advert for a concert by an interviewer. After they have read it, the following questions were asked.

   a) Now that you have had a look at the advert, can you tell me where the concert is being held?

   b) Who will be playing at the concert?

2. The Yellow Pages issued by British Telecom are helpful if we want to locate a business of any kind.

   a) Look at the index papers of the Yellow Pages and tell me which page the details of plumbers is on.

   b) What is the telephone number of a Plumber in the Chiswick area?

Numeracy

1. The cohort member is shown a card with the prices of some food items on it. They have been doing some shopping for a neighbour.

   a) You have bought a loaf of bread (68p) and two tins of soup (45p each). If you are given £2, how much change should you give your neighbour?

2. The cohort member is shown a diagram of a room with its floor measurements. They are asked to calculate the floor area of the room.

Scoring the literacy and numeracy assessments

Each question was coded as correctly answered, incorrectly answered, or not attempted. When a respondent failed to answer three consecutive questions correctly, the assessment was judged to have been completed and no further questions were asked. Three respondents on the literacy assessment and twelve on the numeracy assessment fell into this category. For all the others a score based on aggregating correct answers across all the individual tasks was then calculated separately for literacy and numeracy.

Tests of attainment administered to NCDS cohort at age 7, 11 and 16

At age 7 (1965)

- *Southgate Reading Test* (Southgate, 1962): a test of word recognition and comprehension particularly suited to identifying problems with reading.

- *Copying Designs Test:* a test to obtain some assessment of the child's perceptuo-motor ability.

- *Draw-A-Man Test* (Goodenough, 1926): a test to give some indication of a child's general mental and perceptual ability.

- *Problem Arithmetic Test* (Pringle et al, 1966).

At age 11 (1969)

- *Reading Comprehension Test:* constructed by the National Foundation for Educational Research in England and Wales (NFER) specifically for use in this study.

- *Arithmetic/Mathematics Test:* also constructed by NFER specifically for use in this study.

At age 16 (1974)

- *Reading Comprehension Test:* the same test as that used at age 11.

- *Mathematics Test:* devised at the University of Manchester and originally intended for use in the NFER's study of comprehensive schools.

Tests which are unreferenced have not been published. Copies are available from Social Statistics Research Unit, City University, Northampton Square, London, EC1V 0HB.

The Rutter Scale, (Rutter et al, 1970)

	Certainly Applies (2 pts)	Somewhat Applies (1 pt)	Doesn't Apply (0pts)
1. Very restless, has difficulty staying seated for long	❏	❏	❏
2. Truants from school	❏	❏	❏
3. Squirmy, fidgety	❏	❏	❏
4. Often destroys or damages own or others property	❏	❏	❏
5. Frequently fights or is extremely quarrelsome with other children	❏	❏	❏
6. Not much liked by other children	❏	❏	❏
7. Often worries, worries about many things	❏	❏	❏
8. Tends to be on own – rather solitary	❏	❏	❏
9. Irritable, touchy, is quick to 'fly off the handle'	❏	❏	❏
10. Often appears miserable, unhappy, tearful or distressed	❏	❏	❏
11. Has twitches, mannerisms or tics of the face or body	❏	❏	❏
12. Frequently sucks thumb or finger	❏	❏	❏
13. Frequently bites nails or fingers	❏	❏	❏
14. Tends to be absent from school for trivial reasons	❏	❏	❏
15. Is often disobedient	❏	❏	❏
16. Cannot settle to anything for more than a few moments	❏	❏	❏
17. Tends to be fearful or afraid of new situations and new things	❏	❏	❏
18. Fussy or over particular	❏	❏	❏
19. Often tells lies	❏	❏	❏
20. Has stolen things on one or more occasions in the past 12 months	❏	❏	❏
21. Unresponsive, inert or apathetic	❏	❏	❏
22. Often complains of aches or pains	❏	❏	❏
23. Has had tears on arrival at school or has refused to come into the building in the past 12 months	❏	❏	❏
24. Has a stutter or a stammer	❏	❏	❏
25. Resentful or aggressive when corrected	❏	❏	❏
26. Bullies other children	❏	❏	❏

*A score of 9 or more is representative of a behaviour disorder.

Results of Regression Analyses

Table A4.1: *At birth*

	Literacy		Numeracy	
At birth	*Men*	*Women*	*Men*	*Women*
Age mother left full-time education	.11		.12	.09
Social class at birth (-)	.16	.16	.19	.20
R^2 (% variation explained)	5%	4%	6%	6%

p<.05 unless otherwise stated

Table A4.2: *Up to 7*

	Literacy		Numeracy	
At birth	*Men*	*Women*	*Men*	*Women*
Age mother left full-time education				
Social class at birth (-)	.07	.08	.08	.12
Birthweight				
At age 7				
Reading test	.19	.21	.13	.20
Maths test	.15		.17	.16
Draw-a-man test		.19	.08	.08
Copying design test	.13	.12	.13	.08
Parental interest in education: teacher rated	.09	.10	.08	.09
Mother read to child		.12		.09
School attendance		.06		
Overcrowding in the home (-)	.11		.09	
Rented accommodation				
R^2 (% variation explained)	22%	19%	22%	24%

p<.05 unless otherwise stated

A p-value of p<0.01 indicates that the observed relationship would occur by chance in less than 1% of cases; a p-value of p<0.05 indicates that the observed relationship would occur by chance in less than 5% of cases; A p-value of p<0.1 indicates that the observed relationship would occur by chance in less than 10% of cases.

Table A4.3: *Up to 11*

	Literacy		Numeracy	
	Men	Women	Men	Women
At birth				
Age mother left full-time education				
Social class at birth (-)				.06
Birthweight				
At age 7				
Reading test	.10	.09		.06*
Maths test		.11	.10	.06*
Draw-a-man test			.06*	
Copying Design test	.09	.07	.07	
Parental interest in education:		.08		.05*
teacher rated				
Mother read to child		.10		.06
School attendance		.06	.06	
Overcrowding in the home (-)			.08	
Rented accommodation				
At age 11				
Reading test	.11	.23		.10
Maths test	.14	.14	.30	.35
Parental interest in education:				
teacher rated				
% students in school GCE standard				
School attendance				
Overcrowding in the home (-)	.07*			
Rented accommodation				
Free school meals (-)	.07	.13		.08
R^2 (% variation explained)	26%	27%	29%	34%
*p.<1, otherwise p<.05				

Table A4.4: *Up to 16*

| | Literacy | | Numeracy | |
	Men	Women	Men	Women
At birth				
Age mother left full-time education				
Social class at birth (-)				
Birthweight				
At age 7				
Reading test		.08		.08
Maths test	.07*		.07*	
Draw-a-man test			.06*	
Copying Design test	.10	.06	.07	
Parental interest in education:		.07		
teacher rated				
Mother read to child		.09		.05*
School attendance		.06	.06*	
Overcrowding in the home (-)	.06*		.09	
Rented accommodation				
At age 11				
Reading test		.10		
Maths test		.11	.19	25
Parental interest in education:				
teacher rated				
% students in school GCE standard				
School attendance			.06(-)	
Overcrowding in the home (-)				
Rented accommodation				
Free school meals (-)	.07	.10		.05*.
At age 16				
Reading test	.29	.23	.19	.19
Maths test			.11	.12
Exam score		.10		.09
Parent-Teacher meetings		.06		
Parental interest in education:	.07			
teacher rating				
Single sex school				
Truancy				

continued overleaf

Table A4.4: *continued*	Literacy		Numeracy	
	Men	*Women*	*Men*	*Women*
Rutter score: teacher rated (-)		.07		.09
School attendance				
% dads in school non-manual occupations	.07*			
Rented accommodation				
Overcrowded accommodation				
How many share the bedroom				
R² (% variation explained)	33%	33%	36%	40%
*p<.1 otherwise p<.05				

Table A4.5: *Up to 23*

	Literacy		Numeracy	
	Men	*Women*	*Men*	*Women*
At birth				
Age mother left full-time education				
Social class at birth (-)				
Birthweight				
At age 7				
Reading test	.07*	.07*		
Maths test				
Draw-a-man test			.06	
Copying Design test	.08	.06*		
Parental interest in education:				
teacher rated				
Mother read to child		.08		
School attendance		.05*		
Overcrowding in the home (-)			.08	
Rented accommodation				
At age 11				
Reading test				
Maths test		.10	.18	.24
Parental interest in education:				
teacher rated				
% students in school GCE standard				
School attendance				
Overcrowding in the home (-)				
Rented accommodation				
Free school meals (-)	.07	.09		.05*

continued

Table A4.5: *continued*	Literacy		Numeracy	
	Men	*Women*	*Men*	*Women*
At age 16				
Reading test	.28	.22	.17	.17
Maths test				.13
Exam score				.08
Parent-Teacher meetings		.06		
Parental interest in education: teacher rating	.06*			
Single sex school		.05*		
Truancy				
Rutter score: teacher rated (-)		.06*	.06*	
School attendance				
% dads in school non-manual occupations	.06*			
Rented accommodation				
Overcrowded accommodation		.07*		
How many share the bedroom				
Age 23				
Age left full-time education				
Highest qualification at 23	.17	.16	.18	.08
Work-related training	.07		.07	.05*
Months in employment		.09		
Months unemployed (-)			.12	
Months in f/t home-care (-)				
R^2 (% variation explained)	36%	36%	40%	41%

*p<.1 otherwise p<.05

Table A4.6: *Up to 33*

	Literacy		Numeracy	
	Men	Women	Men	Women
At birth				
Age mother left full-time education				
Social class at birth (-)				
Birthweight				
At age 7				
Reading test	.08*	.07*		
Maths test				
Draw-a-man test			.06	
Copying Design test	.08	.05*		
Parental interest in education: teacher rated				
Mother read to child		.08		.05*
School attendance		.05*	.05*	
Overcrowding in the home (-)			.07	
Rented accommodation				
At age 11				
Reading test		.08*		
Maths test		.10	.17	.25
Parental interest in education: teacher rated				
% students in school GCE standard				
School attendance			.06*	
Overcrowding in the home (-)				
Rented accommodation				
Free school meals (-)	.07	.09		.05*
At age 16				
Reading test	.27	.21	.16	.17
Maths test				.12
Exam score		.07*		.08
Parent-Teacher meetings		.06		
Parental interest in education: teacher rating	.06*			
Single sex school		.05*		
Truancy				

continued

Table A4.6: *continued*	Literacy		Numeracy	
	Men	*Women*	*Men*	*Women*
Rutter score: teacher rated (-)		.06*	.07*	
School attendance				
% dads in school non-manual occupations	.06*			
Rented accommodation				
Overcrowded accommodation				
How many share the bedroom				
Age 23				
Age left full-time education				
Highest qualification at 23		.11		
Work-related training:16-23	.06		.07	
Months in f/t employment:16-23				
Months unemployed:16-23(-)			.11	
Months in f/t home-care: 16-23(-)				
Age 33				
Highest qualification at 33	.15		.17	
Work-related training:23-33				.06*
Months in f/t employment:23-33	.08	.06*	.06	
Months unemployed:23-33 (-)				
Months in f/t home-care:23-33 (-)				
R^2 (% variation explained)	37%	35%	41%	42%
*p<.1 otherwise p<.05				

Predictors of early cognitive skills

Table A5.1: *Reading skills at different ages up to 16*

	Reading at 7		Reading at 11		Reading at 16	
	Men	Women	Men	Women	Men	Women
At birth						
Age mother left full-time education	.09					
Social class at birth (-)				.09		
Birthweight						
At age 7						
Reading test			.36	.28	.07	.07
Maths test			.06	.13	.09	
Draw-a-man test			.05	.13		.05
Copying design test			.12	.11		
Parental interest in education: teacher rated	.25	.27	.09			
Mother read to child			.05*			
School attendance	.14	.10				
Overcrowding in the home (-)	.09	.12				
Rented accommodation		.12	.08(-)			
At age 11						
Reading test					.43	.44
Maths test						
Parental interest in education: teacher rated			.16	.14		
% students in school GCE standard			.13	.08		
School attendance						
Overcrowding in the home (-)					.11	
Rented accommodation						
Free school meals (-)			.05*			.10

continued

Table A5.1: *continued*	Reading at 7		Reading at 11		Reading at 16	
	Men	*Women*	*Men*	*Women*	*Men*	*Women*
At age 16						
Parent-Teacher meetings						
Parental interest in education:					.19	.14
teacher rating						
Single sex school						
Truancy (-)						
Rutter score: teacher rated (-)					.08	.09
School attendance						
% dads in school non-manual occupations					.07	.07
Overcrowded accommodation (-)						
Rented accommodation						.11
How many share the bedroom (-)					.10	
% Variation explained	15%	16%	43%	41%	53%	53%

*=p<.1; p<.05 for all other individual co-efficients; p<.001 for % of overall variation explained

Table A5.2: *Maths skills at different ages up to 16*

| | Maths at 7 | | Maths at 11 | | Maths at 16 | |
	Men	Women	Men	Women	Men	Women
At birth						
Age mother left full-time education	.11					.09
Social class at birth (-)			.06	.07		
Birthweight		.07				
At age 7						
Reading test			.28	.24		
Maths test			.22	.25		.12
Draw-a-man test			.06	.09		
Copying design test			.15	.13		
Parental interest in education: teacher rated	.18	.23	.07			
Mother read to child						
School attendance	.10					
Overcrowding in the home (-)						
Rented accommodation		.10				
At age 11						
Reading test						
Maths test					.43	.33
Parental interest in education: teacher rated			.18	.15		.07
% students in school GCE standard			.14	.13		.07*
School attendance						
Overcrowding in the home (-)			.08(+)			
Rented accommodation						
Free school meals (-)						
At age 16						
Parent-Teacher meetings						
Parental interest in education: teacher rating					.10	.13
Single sex school						.10
Truancy (-)					.08	.11
Rutter score: teacher rated (-)					.12	.08
School attendance						

continued

Table A5.2: *continued*	Maths at 7		Maths at 11		Maths at 16	
	Men	*Women*	*Men*	*Women*	*Men*	*Women*
% dad's in school non-manual occupations					.20	.13
Overcrowded accommodation (-)						
Rented accommodation						
How many share the bedroom (-)						
% Variation explained	8%	9%	50%	45%	53%	48%

*=p<.1; p<.05 for all other individual co-efficients; p<.001 for % of overall variation explained

References

Bynner, J. (in press) Youth and the Information Society, *Journal of Education Policy*.

Bynner, J., Morphy, L. and Parsons, S. (1997) *Women, Employment and Skills*, in Metcalf, H. (ed) *Half our Future: Women, Skill Development and Training*. London: Policy Studies Institute.

Bynner, J. and Parsons, S. (1997a) *It Doesn't Get Any Better: The Impact of Poor Basic Skills on the Lives of 37 year-olds*. London: Basic Skills Agency.

Bynner J. and Parsons, S. (1997b) *Does Numeracy Matter?* London: Basic Skills Agency.

Bynner, J. and Steedman, J. (1995) *Difficulties with Basic Skills*. London: Basic Skills Agency.

Carey, S., Low, S. and Hansbro, J. (1997) *Adult Literacy in Britain*. London: The Stationery Office.

Coffield, F. (1997) *Can the UK Become a Learning Society?*, The Fourth Annual Education Lecture, School of Education, Kings College London.

Ekinsmyth, C. and Bynner, J (1994) *The Basic Skills of Young Adults*. London: Adult Literacy and Basic Skills Unit (ALBSU).

Green, A. and Steedman, H. (1997) *Into the Twenty-First Century: an Assessment of British Skill Profiles*, Special Report, London: Centre for Economic Performance.

Husen, T. (1989) 'Integration of General and Vocational Education', *Education and Vocational Training, CEDFOP, Vocational Training Bulletin* No 1, 9-13.

Industry in Education (1997) *Towards Employability: addressing the Gap between Young People's Qualities and Employer's Recruitment Needs,* Report under the Chairmanship of Sir John Smith, London: Industry in Education.

Lacroix, J-G and Tremblay, G. (1997) 'Conclusion: From Fordism to Gatesism' in Lacroix, J-G and Tremblay, G. 'The Information Society and Cultural Industries Theory', *Current Sociology*, 45, 115-128.